A Diver's Guide To
Northern California

By Bruce Watkins

PUBLISHED BY
SAINT BRENDAN CORP. HOME OF

Saint Brendan Corporation, P.O. Box 11231, Torrance, CA 90510
(310) 792-2333, FAX (310) 792-2336, website: www.saintbrendan.com

Printed in the USA by Rodgers & McDonald Graphics, Carson, CA

SPECIAL NOTE: The descriptions in this book are not scientific facts. The diver's final decisions and actions are their responsibility. The publishers and author of this book assume no responsibility of any mishap claimed to be a result of this book.

ISBN 0-9628600-2-6

Special Thanks to:

Captain Alan Cull
Rocky Daniels of Redwood Empire Divers
Captain Matt, and Marg Hill of Dive Crazy Adventures
Richard Hunter of PacStaR Charters
Joe Jacklavick of NAUI & Valqueros del Mar
John Pepper, the Big Ab Man
Paul Turnbull of Abalone & Marine Resources Council
Ted Wheeler of Aqua Tutus Dive Club
Dan and Laura Wood of Lost Coast Adventures

Dedication:

To Kathleen, who shared the exploration of most of these sites and whose enthusiasm for diving made the experience so much fun.

Contents

Forward

North American Indians believed a person is allotted a certain amount of time at birth, and your life ends when that time passes by. Time spent fishing, however, was not counted toward the total. I firmly believe that the same rule holds true for diving.

Scuba and breath-hold diving are among the most rewarding activities we can enjoy in our watery world. Diving allows us to not only to be on the water, but to be under it, to be part of it, to be one with the sea. Time spent in the water reduces stress, regenerates the mind and body, and nurtures the soul.

The connection to fishing should not be overlooked when discussing California's North Coast diving. No matter how I describe the beautiful and photogenic dive sites of the North Coast, it will be the search for dinner that attracts divers here. Yes, the coastline is of grand and superlative proportions and the reefs are every much as beautiful as Monterey and Southern California (some would claim they are more beautiful). Yet, divers flock here for meat. Spearfishing for lingcod, cabezon and the various species of rockfish attract many each year. However, it is the search of a marine gastropod we call abalone that dominates the diving experience here.

Northern California contains some of the most remote and infrequently dived reefs, and the most densely-packed and diverse marine life in the state of California. Come join me on a tour of some of the most spectacular dive sites in the lower 48 states.

Copper Rockfish

Introduction

In this book I have endeavored to describe most of the California beach diving sites from the Lost Coast of Mendocino south to the Golden Gate Bridge. Besides beach diving I have included a selection of the best sites accessible only via boat. Contained within are the spectacular sites of Mendocino and Sonoma counties, and the seldom visited and mysterious Farallon Islands. I have deliberately excluded sites that require you to trespass to gain entry, and provided expanded details for the more accessible and popular sites of Mendocino and Sonoma Counties.

This part of California is certainly off the beaten path if you are accustomed to Southern California or Monterey beach diving, or hopping on a charter boat to the Channel Islands. In fact, at the time of this writing there are only two dive charter services along the entire North Coast.

This area is seldom visited by divers for many reasons. For the most part the sparse population in the northern part of the state creates a following of local divers with little infusion from Southern California. Unlike the central and southern part of the state there is no lee to hide behind, and there is often no escape from the wind and swell. Reefs here are open to the weather and experience fewer "diver friendly" days than those in the southern part of the state.

Divers here can experience a heightened sense of adventure. These reefs are remote, uncrowded and sometimes require a bit more physical strength to enjoy. Yet on good days these reefs will put most of the world's great reefs to shame. The abundance and diversity of marine life on these northern reefs is hard to beat.

Many of the dive sites described in this book may be located by using mile markers along Highway 1. These mile markers are posted along the highway in both directions and the count runs south to north and begins anew at each county line. So "SON 25" describes a spot 25 miles north of the southern boundary of Sonoma County.

There are currently five dive shops and air stations on the coastline of Sonoma and Mendocino Counties. Sub Surface Progression is a full-service dive shop with a charter boat, and is located on Highway 1, one-quarter mile south of Highway 20 in Fort Bragg, tel. 707-964-3793. Dive Crazy Adventures is a full-service dive shop with a charter boat, and is located in Schooners Landing in Albion, tel. 707-937-3079. Jay Baker Center has an air station and rents and sells breath-hold diving equipment, and is located in Gualala on High-way 1, tel. 707-884-3534. Ocean Cove Store in Sonoma County has an air station on weekends, April through November, and has some dive equipment for sale, tel. 707-847-3422. Bodega Bay Dive Shop is a full service facility and is located on Highway 1 in Bodega Bay, tel. 707-875-3054.

A Brief History of Northern California

Indian Times

Beginning about twelve thousand years ago Northern California was home to Native American Indians, descendants from six linguistic families. Tribes with names like Tolowa, Yurok, Wiyot, Sinkyone, Coast Yuki, Northern and Central Pomo, and Ohlone spread across Northern California.

These Indians lived in harmony with each other and with nature. Wars or tribal fighting was rare, mostly due to the abundance of natural resources. These people were short, but incredibly strong. It was said that they could carry heavy baskets for many miles throughout the coastal mountains.

Unlike their counterparts to the north and south, Northern California Indians never developed seafaring skills. The Tolowa and Yurok of Del Norte County built crude dugout canoes to navigate rivers and near-shore ocean waters, while the southern tribes built simple rafts to cross rivers or to travel to offshore rocks to hunt sea lions.

These people migrated each year between their winter and summer villages. Summers were spent along the coast where they gathered abalone, clams, mussels, kelp, and salt. Fish were caught with nets, and marine mammals were hunted with clubs. Much of this food was salted and dried to preserve it through the winter. During the winter they migrated inland to harvest acorns, and to hunt deer and bear.

Usually, food was boiled before it was eaten. This was a somewhat difficult task for these Indians since they lacked the technology to make pottery. They were, however, superb weavers and developed the skill to weave baskets that were water-tight. Abalone and other dried foods were boiled for several hours, and cooking was accomplished by the addition of fire heated rocks, one at a time. This was a time consuming process, requiring the better part of the day to prepare dinner. The skill of these weavers and the beauty of their baskets were renowned throughout North America.

European exploration and settlement

The first European to gaze on Northern California was probably Sir Francis Drake in 1542, although he did not document his landings very well. Spanish Explorers sent out numerous exploratory/ mapping expeditions during the mid 1600s and 1700s and named most of the headlands. In 1595 Sebastian Cermeno wrecked his ship the *San Agustin* north of Mendocino and rowed to Acapulco. He gave the name "La Bahia de San Francisco" the bight South of Point Reyes. In 1602 Sebastián Vizcaíno charted much of California, but missed the Golden Gate. It was not until 1775 that Juan Manuel de Ayala became the first European to enter and explore San Francisco Bay.

The Spanish established settlements around good seaports and suitable mining and framing areas. Presidios, fortified garrisons of troupes, offered protection to these settlements and Spanish economic interests. Twenty-one Missions were added along the famed El Camino Real (The Royal Road) from San Diego north to Sonoma, including Monterey, Santa Cruz, and San Francisco. Their most northerly settlements were the Mission San Francisco Solano with a presidio near the present day town of Sonoma, and Rancho Punta de los Reyes (Point Reyes, Point of the Kings), and Rancho Tomales y Baulenes (Tomales and Bolinas Bays).

In these missions the local Indian populations were rounded up and labored on Spanish farms and ranches. Separated from their historic food supplies and provided with only what the Spanish had left over, the Indians experienced hunger for the first time. Although there were several unsuccessful revolts, the Indian way of life and the people themselves succumbed to a combination of interbreeding the Spanish and European diseases for which they had no immunity.

During the 1800s, while the Spanish were extending their boundaries north through Monterey and San Francisco, Russians settlements spread south from Alaska and Washington. Russian fur traders established a settlement at Bodega Bay in 1809. Nearby Spanish strongholds intimidated the Russians, so in 1812 they retreated and established their main settlement 30 miles north. At Fort Ross they built a small fort with stockade, surrounded by a village.

The Spanish were not particularly fond of their Russian neighbors but never made an attempt to take the fort. This was partially due to the secure placement of the stockade high above the beach. It may also have been due to the alliances the Russians formed with the local Indian tribes. The Alaskan Indians that the Russians first contacted were superb seafarers and hunters. The Russians learned early on that they were better off if they worked with local tribes. Russians always used local Indian labor, most by conscription, but paid the Indians, allowing them to practice their historic religion, and treating them well by the standards of the time. The Pomo tribes of Sonoma County gladly formed alliances with the Russians rather than submit to the treatment that the southern tribes experienced at the hands of the Spanish.

The Russians withdrew in 1841 when the sea otter became virtually extinct and other marine mammals were no longer worth hunting. They left little to remember them by, just the remains of a fort and several names on the map.

During the early 1840s California began to be settled by the first U.S. citizens. These were mostly farmers, but some were traders and whalers. Conflicts soon developed between Spanish and U.S. settlers. The Spanish American War of 1846 brought this conflict to a head and the treaty of Guadalupe in 1848 established the current U.S.- Mexican border. This act started California down the road to statehood, which was granted in 1850.

It was somewhat prophetic that only after the end of the war did a mill worker named James W. Marshall find a little gold nugget at John Sutter's mill on the American River. With the discovery gold came a wave of people that swept across the state and changed the landscape forever.

Dog-Hole Times

In the mid to late 1800s if you wanted to visit Northern California you would not travel by automobile, locomotive, or horse. The population was too sparse and the terrain too rugged to justify bringing either roads or rail to these remote, coastal locations. The only way to get there was by ship.

Unlike the Eastern United States, the West Coast lacked good harbors and was under a prevailing northwesterly wind and swell. This combination proved unappealing if not downright dangerous to early sea travelers. Up until about 1850, few ships plied the waters of the North Coast. In 1847 only two brigs, the *Henry* and the *Janet*, carried cargo between the Columbia River and San Francisco, and they went via Honolulu.

That all changed during the late 1840s. As late as 1845, San Francisco was a tiny village of no more than 300 people, and the bay area was little more than a way point for fur traders and explorers. By 1853 San Francisco had jumped to a city of 150,000. They needed wood to build a city and food to feed its people. Since there was little of

Fort Ross.

either locally, San Francisco looked elsewhere. A simple navigation error and the resulting salvage effort turned San Francisco's attention to the North Coast.

The *Frolic* left Bombay during the spring of 1850, made a stop in Hong Kong, and headed for San Francisco. On July 26 the Frolic miscalculated her location and wound up on the rocks in a little cove just north of the present-day Caspar Lighthouse. When word reached San Francisco of the wreck and her cargo of silks and china, a team was dispatched by Henry Meiggs to recover what they could. They brought back no treasure since the coastal Indians had picked over what they wanted. More important than treasure, however, they brought back stories of huge forests with enormous trees.

At that time redwood forests stretched from Russian Gulch in Sonoma County northward into Oregon. It was reported that, "The forests up in that area have no end. A medium-sized tree could provide enough lumber to build one-half dozen churches." This was Paul Bunyan's Country.

And, a beautiful country it was. Three-hundred-foot high redwoods covered the hills and ran right to the coastal cliffs. Six-foot ferns were dwarfed by the huge trees. The habitat supported herds of deer and elk, along with river otters, grizzly bears, and mountain lions. The rugged, fog-shrouded coast must have been inspiring to those who first saw it from land.

I bet that those who first attempted to approach the Mendocino coast from the sea did not appreciate the beauty quite so much. Vertical cliffs, a rocky coast full of "widow makers," a prevailing northwesterly wind, and no real harbors made the North Coast a treacherous place to sail. Yet the race for timber was on.

Saw mills and ports sprang up on every available site from the Russian River north. The lack of good ports made shipping a touch-and-go operation. The ships would anchor, load up, and leave before the weather changed. Little nooks in the coastline had to suffice for ports. These were called dog-hole ports. No one knows the exact origin of the term. Some say that a proper dog would not be caught in one. Others claim that when a captain first sighted his port-of-call he exclaimed that, "There was not enough room for a dog to turn around in, let alone a sailing vessel."

Numerous types of vessels initially tried to utilize these minimal anchorages, but the small ports and prevailing wind made things difficult. Ships that were small enough to anchor in the dog-holes had a hard time with the uphill run out of San Francisco.

The best solution was the schooner. These ships were small, all grossed under 200 tons and most under 100 tons. They had a mast both fore and aft, a sharp bow and rounded stern. The dog-holers were fast enough to beat into a prevailing wind, and could turn on a dime. The only real dog-holer was a schooner.

These rugged ships were captained by rugged and seasoned sailors, mostly from Sweden, Norway, Finland, and Denmark. As a result the dog-holers were often referred to as the "Scandinavian Navy." These guys were superb seamen. Once a lady passenger asked one captain how he could find their port in a pea-soup fog. The skipper snapped, "Why, I've been there before!" Modesty ran high with these captains.

Sometimes it had to. All too often the mill owner's wife or daughter would ask the captain to pick up a few things to pretty up the house from San Francisco, and only the Old Man himself would do. Many a captain got a fat lip or a black eye over what the rough crowd at the San Francisco waterfront thought was "proper" for a "real" man to buy.

Ships made money mostly on the timber they hauled. Their hulls were packed as tightly as possible and more timber was lashed to the deck. These seemingly overloaded ships were in no danger of sinking since wood floats, and it was said that the ships ran smoother when their decks were awash. On her first lumber run between the Colombia River and San

Point Arena.

Francisco the *Sequin* netted twenty-thousand dollars. That was a lot of money in those days.

The schooners were mostly empty when they headed north out of San Francisco, and carried either rocks for ballast or light cargo to stock the general store at the mill. Most of the ships carried a handful of passengers, but they were always secondary to the cargo.

These ships were always at the mercy of the weather as they could only enter and leave ports when the wind allowed. Since the wind was mostly northwesterly, getting out of a port was harder than getting into one. Once the *Mindora* had to lay off the Colombia river for nearly a month before favorable winds would allow her to cross the bar. The captain thought his ship was safely at anchor in the harbor when the current grabbed the ship, hurled her to the beach and broke her back.

About 1880 some ingenious chap put a steam engine on a sailing ship and created the first "steam schooner." These ships still had sails in case the engine failed to start and to save on fuel. Coal was expensive at that time, since it was imported from the east. Steamers could head directly into the wind and leave port when the captain wanted rather when the wind was right. These unsightly ships ruled the coast for the next 50 years.

Sailing captains and crews resented the conversions and fights between the sailing and steam crew members were common. The norm was to have the engine operators remain below deck while the rest of the crew wandered around above deck wondering what to do. The sailors had little to do when the steam engines were driving the ship.

Lumber mills sprang up at the mouth of every river and most streams from Jenner, at the mouth of the Russian River, northward. Most mills had an associated anchorage, and most of these were no more than a small nook in the coastline. These were dog-hole ports. In total there were 69 dogholes in Northern California and 65 of these were in present day Sonoma and Mendocino counties.

Often the ports were named after the mill owner: Haven's Anchorage or Stewart's Point. Others were named for the local geography: Little River, Big River or Salt Point. Still others were named out of the frustration of anchoring there: Hard Scratch Landing, Rough and Ready, or Nip and Tuck.

Lumber was the primary, if not only, export of these ports; although game meat, potatoes and later beef became major commodities. A little town sprang up around each mill and contained a general store, saloon, and mill offices. The larger towns had a hotel or two.

Most of the lumbermen were Swedes, who were paid every six months. The saloons would cash the men's checks and the big Swedes would drink until their money ran out. They would then sober up and head back into the woods for another six months.

Stands of timber near the mill were logged first, followed by a path up stream. When the stream bed was logged as far back as one could float a log, oxen trains were used to drag the timber to the mills. When that was not practical, the stream beds were dammed, and the beds filled with cut logs. After the first good rain of the season the dam was dynamited and the logs shot down the bed all the way to the mill. Of course, if it rained a bit more than expected, the logs shot past the mill and out to sea. Often an entire season of logging was lost that way.

Initially, logs were loaded onto ships by floating them out to waiting ships. As you might expect, this was a very time-consuming process as the logs were picked out of the water one at a time. Later, slide chutes were erected on the north side of many dog hole ports, and lumber, one piece at a time, was slid down the chute onto the deck of an anchored ship. This method was, of course, useless to unload ships.

A few ports, notably Albion and Little River, did manage to build wharves big enough to handle lumber ships. Big storm waves and the lack of protected anchorages meant that many of these wharves lasted only a single season at best, and often not even that long.

After the Civil War, high quality wire became available and small steam engines (known as donkey engines) became common. This allowed efficient loading and unloading of ships "under the wire." A piece of high tension wire was anchored to the sea bed and the other end onshore. A counterweighted traveler carried bundles of wood onto the ship and cargo back. The donkey engines made the task easier and lumber could be handled in bundles instead of one piece at a time. That meant ships could be loaded a lot faster.

Speed was often needed. The weather along the north coast is not known for its placidness and could change at a moment's notice. Loading and unloading was a touchy job, and captains did not want to spend a moment longer at anchor than they absolutely had to.

Most chutes and high wires were on the north side of coves to offer the most protection from the northwesterly swell. When the wind switched to come out of the south the ships had to leave port

Dive Site Rating

I have adopted a system from my ski buddies to rate these dive sites. A beginner site (●) is one for a newly certified diver, or one who has not put on a tank for some time, or a diver who has little/no experience in California beach diving. These sites are not likely to get them into trouble. They have parking near the entry point and have predictably calm and less strenuous entries and exits. These sites are mostly in protected coves but the beginner rating needs to be upgraded when the swell is running straight into the cove or when diving near the cove mouth.

Intermediate sites (■) are ones that should only be attempted if you have recent California beach diving experience and are in reasonably good physical shape. Beginners should be comfortable here if they are with a more experienced diver.

Advanced sites (◆) should only be attempted by experienced California divers who are in good physical shape. There may be strenuous walks to the entry point or difficult beach/rock entries. Experience in reading ocean conditions is a must.

Difficult sites (◆◆) should only be attempted by the most knowledgeable/experienced California divers who are in excellent physical condition. These sites are characterized by difficult/strenuous entries and exits, often have long walks to the entry point, and have rough surface conditions and strong currents. Experienced divers should not bring novice divers along on these dives.

Note: Weather will influence the above rating system. A storm swell can turn the easiest entry into a double black diamond in less than an hour. Take some time to evaluate the conditions and determine if you are comfortable with the conditions at a specific site on a specific day. It is always better to use your experience to choose not to dive, rather than rely on strength and skill to get you out of difficult situations.

These ratings are only applicable to beach entries. Those diving from their own boats should evaluate the conditions of the day against their own experiences. Passengers on charter boats should seek guidance from the boat's captain.

Thoughts on California Weather

Divers tend to think of California weather in three distinct diving seasons. During the spring and summer the Central Valley gradually heats up, drawing air and moisture off the ocean. These conditions produce steady, northwesterly winds, foggy beaches, and strong upwelling.

fast as the big California storms have southerly winds. Sailing ships were often forced to remain at port during these sudden storms and all the captain could do was hope that his anchor did not drag. Many a proud ship was reduced to splinters in these dog-holes.

The heyday of the dog hole schooner began to wane when most of the lumber was taken out, and the great depression reduced the demand for building materials. The transcontinental railroad was completed in 1869, but it was not until 1876 that the Southern Pacific Railroad would complete the line between San Francisco and Los Angeles, and not until 1912 that a line would run from Fort Bragg to Willits in Mendocino County. Only during the 1930s did paved roads become commonplace in California.

It was only then that the dog-holers no longer had a place. And, a sad day it was. Somehow the image of an 18-wheeler twisting along Highway 1 does not conjure up the same feelings as a two-masted schooner on a uphill run along the Redwood Coast. The rugged individualism of the dog-hole crew remains today in the few fisherpersons that call the old dog-hole ports home.

The coastline near Elk.

Dive Site Ratings

DIVE SITE	SITE RATING	VISIBILITY	FACILITIES	GAME	ACCESS	ENTRY
MENDOCINO COUNTY						
Usal	◆	P	T, BL, C	VG	E	D
Westport/Union Landing	◆	P	T, C, S, BL, LP	VG	M, VD	D,VD
Kibesillah	■	F	N	VG	D	M
MacKerricher State Park	■	F	T	F	E, M	M
Glass Beach	■	F	N	G	M	M
Noyo Cove	●	F	T, BR	G	E	E, LS
Hare Creek	●	G	N, LP	G	M	M
Jug Handle State Reserve	■	G	T	VG	M	E, LS
Caspar Cove	■	G	T	VG, R	E	E, LS
Russian Gulch State Park	●	G	T, C, S, BL	G	E,D	E,D
500D	◆◆	G	N, LP	G	D,VD	D
Mendocino Headlands State Park	◆	G	T	G	D, VD	
Van Damme State Park	●	G	T, C, S, BL	F	E	E
Buckhorn cove	●	G	N, LP	G	M	E
Albion	●	G	T, C, S, BR, DS	G	E	E, LS
Navarro River Beach	◆	P	T, C, BL	G	E	D
Elk	◆◆	F	T, LP	VG	VD, SC	E
Arena Cove	●	F	T, S, BR	F	E	E
Arena Rock	Boat Only	VG	N	VG	B	B
Anchor Bay	●	G	T, C, S, BL	G	E	E
Collins Landing	■	G	N, LP	G	M	M
SONOMA COUNTY						
Pebble Beach	■	F	T, LP	G	M	M
Horseshoe cove	◆	F	N, LP	G	D, SC	E
Kruse Ranch	◆	F	N, LP	G	D	VD
Fisk Mill Cove	■	F	T	G	D	M
South Cove	■	F	N, LP	G	M	M
Stump Beach	■	F	T	F	M	M
Gerstle Cove	●	F	T, C, S, BL	R	M	E
South Gerstle Cove	■	F	T	G	M	M
Ocean Cove	●	F	T, C, S, BL	G	M	E, M
Stillwater Cove	●	F	T, C, S, BL	G	E	E
Cemetery Reef	Boat Only	G	N	G	B	B
Timber Cove	●	F	T, C, S, BL	G	E	E
Fort Ross State Historical Park	■	F	T, BL	G	E, M	E
Fort Ross Reef	◆	P	T, C	G	VD, SC	D
Russian Gulch	◆	P	T	P	M	M
MARIN/SAN FRANCISCO CO.						
Tomales Point	Boat Only	P	N	G	B	B
Abalone Point/Double Point	◆◆	P	T	G	VD, SC	D
Noonday Rock	Boat Only	VG	N	VG	B	B
Isle of St. James	Boat Only	VG	N	VG	B	B
Middle Farallon	Boat Only	VG	N	VG	B	B
Southeast Farallon	Boat Only	VG	N	VG	B	B

● BEGINNER SITE
■ INTERMEDIATE SITE
◆ ADVANCED SITE
◆◆ DIFFICULT SITE
P POOR
F FAIR
G GOOD
VG VERY GOOD
T TOILETS

LP LIMITED PARKING
B BOAT DIVE ONLY
E EASY
M MODERATE
D DIFFICULT
VD VERY DIFFICULT
BL BOAT LAUNCH
(for kayaks and small inflatables)
BR BOAT RAMP (for larger boats)

LS LONG SWIM
SC STRENUOUS CLIMB
LP LIMITED PARKING
S SHOWERS
C CAMPING
R RESERVE/NO HUNTING
DS DIVE SHOP

Upwelling occurs when winds drive surface water out to sea to be replaced by cold, nutrient-laden waters from deep below. This upwelling brings together two essential factors together, sunlight and nutrients, and the plankton thrives.

During spring and summer the surface temperatures can drop to a chilly 43-45 degrees and the water turns the color and turbidity of green pea soup. Or the water may turn a deep red due to the presence of specific types of dinoflagelets, a condition that is often called a "red tide." This upwelling and the resulting explosion of life is what makes California marine life so diverse and rich.

During late summer through fall the northwesterly winds wane, and the water temperature climbs to its highest yearly values (high 50s to mid 60s during particularly warm years). This is the predictably best time to dive Northern California. The visibility can generally be counted on to be quite good (30 to 60 feet) and the wind and wave action are very acceptable. Beaches are likely to be clear and sunny.

Winter can best be characterized as beauty and the beast. When the winter storms roll through California with their 70-mile-per-hour plus winds and 18-foot swells, it is best to view the ocean from a long, safe distance. However, the times between storms produce the absolutely finest conditions of the year. The sun is low in the sky, providing minimal light for water-clouding plankton. At times the visibility may grow to 70 feet and occasionally over 100 feet, and the water temperature will hover in the 50s. On these days Northern California will put highly rated tropical locations to shame.

On balance, the weather on the coast is highly changeable and somewhat unpredictable. Every now and then the little demons that mess with our weather do something really funky. At times their playfulness can result in spectacular disasters, but other times can produce some mighty fine diving. For instance El Niño conditions (a warm, northward running current that occurs irregularly) can produce superior conditions with warm, clear water and an assortment of interesting critters brought up from Southern California. El Niño can also result in a continuous stream of big storms.

Beach Diving Tips

First and foremost, diving is supposed to be fun! If you get in over your head and push your physical abilities, you are probably not having fun. Know yourself, your abilities and interests. Then decide if you will enjoy the dive at hand. It is perfectly all right to drive three hours to a site and blow off the dive off due to non-optimal ocean conditions.

Typically, waves break on the beach in sets, several small waves followed by a set of larger waves. Take twenty minutes or so to watch the ocean so you get a an understanding of how the waves are breaking that day, and how large the largest wave is likely to be. The self control to sit and watch, rather than immediately jump into your gear and go, may save you a good thrashing at the hands of an uncaring ocean.

Divers should enter during the periods of smaller waves. Enter the water with your regulator in your mouth, and turn and swim away from the beach. The trick is to traverse the surf line as quickly as possible. When exiting, again have your regulator in your mouth and crawl until you are well out of the surf line. This technique is known by locals as "The Monastery Crawl."

Divers who are experienced with sandy beach entries may find rocky point entries a little scary the first time around, but become adept at it very quickly. Simply wait for the swell to come up to its maximum point, one giant stride and two kicks later you are in deep water and far from the rocks. Take a little time to observe the area into which you intend to jump. The last thing you want to do is to skewer yourself on a rock that is lurking just below the surface.

Divers enter the water at Jack Peters Cove.

Rocky beach exits are often easier in moderate waves than sandy beach exits. Simply swim up to the ledge with your regulator in your mouth and allow a wave to carry you up onto the rocks. Once on the rocks, either a short crawl or two steps will put you out of reach of the ocean. This is a lot easier than it sounds.

Beach divers are pushed back and forth by wave action and must expel a fair amount of effort getting through the surf line. On rocky entries the energy of the wave is directed up and down and tends to pick you up rather than smash you against the rocks. On particularly rough days you will want to watch the wave pattern before approaching the rocks, and pick a time where the sets are at a low intensity. Alternatively, on calm days you will want to ride the largest wave out of the water. A little experience in timing waves will allow you to get in and out with a surprising small amount of effort.

Remember, you are ultimately responsible for your safety, and your diving skills need to be weighed against the conditions de jour.

Northern California Reef Community: Abalone, Urchins and Kelp

The inshore reef communities of Northern California are dominated by enormous beds of bull kelp *(Nereocystis luetkeana)*. Bull kelp is streamlined and is able to survive on the exposed northern coasts with their sometimes rough waters. The giant kelp *(Macrocystis pyrifera)* is common to southern waters and has more frond area per plant. This design is efficient at capturing sunlight, but offers so much resistance to water movement that these plants are easily ripped out by moderate Nor Cal storms. This is not to say you won't find giant kelp in Northern California; you'll probably just find it in sheltered coves.

These kelp beds are primarily preyed upon by abalone and two species of urchin. The abalone and urchin have different feeding habits and moderate the size of the kelp beds in different ways. Abalone primarily feed on bits of the kelp canopy that have broken off and drift along the sea floor. They often feed simply by lifting part of their foot and wait for a piece of kelp to drift underneath. They also actively forage, particularly at night.

Divers can take advantage of this behavior and loosen abalone from rocks by gently touching a piece of kelp to the ab's tentacles. The ab will

Abalone and urchins.

A diver explores the kelp forest.

Urchins.

rear up and try to capture the kelp. This is not an urban legend, but a exhibition of an abalone's programmed, feeding behavior.

Urchins feed on drifting kelp but also aggressively feed on kelp holdfasts. Once the holdfast is weakened the entire plant breaks away and becomes entangled in the kelp canopy. When enough of the kelp plants have become detached, the action of wind and waves can rip out an entire bed.

Prior to the influx of Europeans the sea otter was the principal predator that kept populations of abalone and urchins in balance. There has not been a sea otter sighted on these northern reefs for over 150 years and the lack of predators has allowed the abalone and urchins to grow beyond historic levels. The enormous populations of abalone that Northern California divers have grown accustomed to are a direct result of the removal of the sea otters.

In modern times the sport abalone fishery has constrained the abalone population somewhat, but commercial urchin fishing has had a bigger impact. Intense commercial fishing for urchins during the past decade has effectively removed one of the kelp's major predators from some locations. In these areas the kelp beds are growing thicker. This urchin fishery seems to have a positive effect on the abalone fishery. The thicker kelp beds keeps the abalone spawn inshore and deposit more baby abalone in suitable habitats, and with the removal of urchins there is more food and space for the abalone. Simply put, in many areas there are more abalone now than 20 years ago.

Marine Mammals

Of all of the animals in California waters the marine mammals seem to get the most attention from non-divers. Seals and sea lions are common to Northern California and are referred to in scientific terms as pinnipeds, which means "feather feet," referring to their flat fin feet. These marine mammals are often confused but are easily distinguished with a little practice. Sea lions belong to the family Otariidae and have a small external ear and are sometimes referred to as eared seals. But true seals, of the family Phocidae, lack an external ear. A seal in the water will submerge by backing down, while a sea lion will propel itself down nose first. Sea lions use their large and powerful fore flippers for propulsion through the water and seals will use their hind flippers. Sea lions have hind flippers,

which may be turned forward, and in combination with their strong fore flippers allows them to walk or waddle on land. The hind flippers of seals can not be turned forward and they move on land with an awkward, worm-like motion.

Of all of the marine mammals in California, harbor seals *(Phoca vitulina)* seem to be the most friendly and frequently choose to approach divers. At times they will play with or harass divers, depending on your perspective. Spearfishing around seals is a dumb idea. The seal will almost always get your catch. It is illegal to deliberately feed any marine mammal, but if they steal from you, I guess it was their fish in the first place. They are, however, great fun to watch underwater. Remember it is illegal to chase marine mammals. The better photographs and more memorable encounters happen when a brain-damaged (e.g., cooperative) mammal chooses to play with you.

Harbor seals feed on octopus, squid, shellfish, and small fish. They usually hunt in the early morning hours and then spend the rest of the day sleeping on offshore rocks. Harbor seals are promiscuous and do not form harems as do sea lions. Pupping occurs in March through May on isolated beaches throughout the state. These cute little fur balls are capable of swimming from birth and are heart-lifting to watch as they nurse, or sleep in the sun, or frolic in the near-shore waters. The mother only cares for the young seal for a few weeks and will often leave the pup alone on the beach for an hour or so while she is hunting. Good intentioned beach combers often rescue these "abandoned" seals. It's best to leave them untouched and allow the mother to reclaim her pup. MacKerricher State Park, Pebble Beach at The Sea Ranch, the beaches south of Fort Ross to Goat Rock State Beach at the mouth of the Russian River are good places to view harbor seals.

Harbor seal.

Elephant seals *(Mirounga angustirostris)* spend much of their life at sea. They are the champion deep divers in the world of mammals and regularly dive to 3500 feet! In early winter elephant seals haul out in massive herds for pupping and mating. They form large harems with one alpha male in charge. The male of the species has an enormous nose that is inflated and acts as a sounding board. Their nasal trumpeting can heard for miles and is used to attract mates and to intimidate other males from entering their territory. When the trumpeting fails to ward off a rival male, the two often engage in bloody fighting. These duels rarely result in the death of a seal, but do leave their necks scarred. Southeast Farallon Island and Año Nuevo State Reserve are good places to see Elephant Seals. Año Nuevo State Reserve offers organized "seal walks." Call 650-879-0227 or on the web "www.anonuevo.org," for more information.

Sea lions often announce their presence with barking that can be heard for some distance both above and below the water. Divers can get a close- up look of the herd as the sea lions sun themselves and an even closer look underwater. While normally shy when on land, the sea lions are at home in the water and lose much of their fear of men. They will spend long hours playing games of hide-and-seek with divers and blowing bubbles in their faces. There is no need to chase after these mammals (in addition to being illegal) as they will certainly come to you. One of my techniques for getting sea lion photographs is to pretend to be interested in something else—a hole or a rock. More often than not a sea lion will come right up to me and peer over my shoulder in order to see what I'm looking at.

California sea lions *(Zalophus californianus)* breed of offshore islands during the late spring and summer, so you should not expect to see many along the coast from May through August. Afterwards the adults, along with juveniles, return to their regular haulouts. Sea lions generally feed at night and spend most of the day resting and sleeping. Weighing between 500 and 750 pounds, they sometimes form large groups floating on the surface with one flipper in the air. The flipper acts as a solar collector to warm the sea lion. Fish rocks at Anchor Bay, and Southeast Farallon Island are good places to view sea lions.

Stellar sea lions *(Eumetopias jubatus)* also haul out at these locations. They are larger than California sea lions, weigh up to 2000 pounds and have a yellowish-brown fur coat when dry, but are silvery when wet. Stellars are much less common than California sea lions, are generally less noisy, and males lack the high bony forehead (saggital crest) typical of male California sea lions.

Gray whales *(Eschrictius robustus)* migrate past California twice each year as they travel between their feeding grounds in Alaska and their breeding grounds in Mexico. Grays are benthic (bottom) feeders and sift soft sand and mud bottoms for crustacean and other bottom dwellers. During their migrations they rarely feed. Their southerly migrations begins in late fall and lasts through February. During this southerly move they remain far out to sea and only come close to shore at prominent, westerly points of land. The migration peaks for about two weeks, normally during early January. During the northerly migration, which lasts from February through June, the migrating whales tend to hug the coastline. Divers rarely encounter whales while underwater, but often see them on their way to and from dive sites. Point Reyes, Point Arena, Salt Point, and Mendocino Headlands are all good places to watch whales.

Sea lion.

Elephant seal.

Sharks

The most common shark in Northern California is the blue shark *(Prionace glauca)*. Blues are nothing short of poetry in motion. With a minimum of body movement they effortlessly glide through the water and their iridescent color sparkles in the sunlight. A blue's behavior towards divers is one of restrained curiosity rather than aggression and most divers thoroughly enjoy the experience.

Shortfin mako sharks *(Isurus oxyrhincus)* are probably not more dangerous than a blue, but they look frightening. Their mouth is agape with jagged teeth pointing in every direction (surely an orthodontist's nightmare). They are also a fast and nervous shark. One minute they are in front of you, the next they are behind you. Diving with makos is exciting.

On rare occasions divers encounter the great white shark *(Charcharodon* carcharius). Whites hunt inshore animals and are commonly found in shallow water near marine mammal haul-outs. Underwater a diver can only be amazed with the size and power of a white. They are thick, heavy- bodied animals that are incredibly impressive when viewed either from above or below the water. A diver is truly lucky to get a glimpse of these animals.

Diver's often ask how to avoid being bitten by a shark. The only true shark repellent is the shade of an oak tree (oak trees don't grow near salt water). Which is another way of saying don't go near the water if you're afraid of sharks. On the other hand divers are rarely bitten by sharks and you are certainly at greater risk of becoming involved in an automobile accident driving to the dive site than being bitten by a shark. Also, sharks rarely bite more than once, so dive with a buddy and they can pull you to safety should the improbable happen.

My best advice to avoid shark attack is not to dive at locations where shark attacks are common. Many speak of a "red triangle" where shark attacks are more common (Point Reyes to the Farallon Islands to Año Nuevo Island). I believe it is more reasonable to suggest that large sharks will be found near to what they eat, and there are large concentrations of marine mammals, and particularly elephant seals, at these locations. The three areas also happen to define a triangle. These and near-by sites should be avoided if you are concerned about shark attack. California Fish and Game divers and many research divers are forbidden by their employers to dive in these areas. Yet many divers visit these sites and never see a shark. In a total of 14 diving days at the Farallon Islands our group spotted only one white shark. This shark

Blue shark.

show no interest whatsoever in our scuba divers. These trips were planned to avoid the time when large numbers of elephant seals were on the Islands (September to January), since elephant seals are one of the white shark's favorite foods. You must make up your own mind on if and when to dive these areas.

It is tempting to try to correlate shark bites with the activity of the victim, but in reality there is too little data available to draw hard conclusions. Since 1926 there have been 35 shark attacks on humans from the Golden Gate north to Oregon, and only one of those attacks was fatal. Out of the 35 attacks, 17 have been on free divers and 11 of those were from the Point Reyes/Bodega Bay area. There were six attacks on scuba divers, four of those at the Farallon Islands. There were seven attacks on surfers, and most of those occurred in Humboldt and Del Norte Counties. Most of these attacks occurred from the beginning of August through the end of October. More than anything else, attacks correlate with numbers of people in the water. As the number of people taking up diving, surfing, swimming, and other water sports increases, there will be more shark attacks simply because there is a greater number of people in the water.

A free-diver uses an ab iron to pull an abalone.

Game Diving Tips

Catching one's dinner is a popular diving activity throughout California. Divers should recognize that the ocean's bounties are not endless and they should take game responsibly. In a time of dwindling resources, killing for killing's sake is no longer acceptable. Divers should be aware of Department of Fish and Game Laws, and follow them. Beyond these laws there is a code of honor among divers that should be followed. Take only what you intend to eat, and eat what you take. Never shoot a fish if you are unsure that it is good to eat. Only shoot fish that you have both the equipment and skill to land. Remember, leaving a wounded fish to slowly die will get no one a medal of honor. Attempting to land a 50-pounder with a pole spear will only get the spear broken, yourself injured, and will probably end up feeding a group of sea stars when the wounded animal finally dies. Fish are best shot just behind the head and they should be placed on a stringer as soon as possible to avoid losing them. They may be strung either through the gills or eye sockets. Larger speared fish can often be subdued by grasping their eye sockets.

Abalone

The single most important thing that motivates divers in Northern California is the search for abalone or simply "abs." The waters off Northern California continue to produce a bountiful harvest of these mollusks, and with a little care and conservation they will continue to do so well into the future.

While there a great many species of abalone world-wide there is only one species commonly observed in Northern California. The red abalone *(Haliotis rufescens)* is the world's largest abalone and thrives in cold waters from Oregon to Baja.

Abalone are actually primitive snails. Their digestive tract is arranged in circular fashion around the shell and their mouth is located very near their anus. Abalone are considered primitive animals because they defecate on their own head. Apparently, it was a major step in evolution to separate the two parts.

There are girl abalone and boy abalone. The largest and most conspicuous organ in both sexes is the reproductive gland; the boys are pink and the girls are blue-green. Abalone are broadcast spawners; that is, individuals release eggs and sperm into the water. Abalone have a complex chemical trigger that ensures that nearby individuals release their spawn at the same time. There are a number of

In Search of the 10-Inch Abalone

So you've been diving a while, can free-dive 30 feet, and have no trouble getting your limit of four abalone in a few free dives. But now you want some really big abs, and we are not talking nine inchers. You want a trophy. Veteran ab diver Ted Wheeler of Aqua Tutus Dive Club offers a little insight. And his advice should be heeded, for he is one of the most successful trophy ab hunters in the state. With his limits of 10-inchers (that's four abalone in a single day whose size exceeded 10 inches) and a total of 60 abs over 10 inches under his belt, he is an ab diver, par excellence.

Ted's advice is to scout an area before you dive and look in areas that are normally too rough to dive, but are currently diveable. "Look for area that has old abs, ones whose shells are riddled with holes from boring marine parasites. Take a measuring device that will allow you to gauge the size of the big abs and don't spend any time messing with the tiny nine-inchers." A boat helps to get you to these remote areas and most trophies are found in only 10 to 15 feet of water. If the area is not presenting any big abs, choose another location.

Where one big ab is found, another will be close-by. Ted says that big abs are often found in dirty water, and on boulders in sand, and never in an area with a lot of loose rocks. Storm-driven rocks break abalone shells.

Once a suitable area is found Ted will systematically search with help of two marker floats. The first marks the center of the search area, and the other is a floating line attached to his ab gauge to allow him to mark the location of a 10-incher should he run out of breath and need to make a second dive. Many use a 40-foot piece of plastic tubing to attach their float to their abalone iron.

factors that affect the efficiency of spawning. One is the local density of abalone, more abalone in one place ensures a greater probability that eggs and sperm will unite. For this reason it is better if ab divers do not clean out a "glory hole," but rather leave a number of abalone together to maximize the baby abalone that they will produce.

Other factors are currents and kelp bed thickness. If the currents are strong the spawn may be taken out to sea and the juvenile abalone may never find a suitable habitat to attach themselves. A thick kelp bed ensures that the larva will have sufficient in-shore time to develop before baby abalone must find their spot on the reef. Baby abalone, by-the-way, prefer to feed on red coralline algae.

Abalone are hemophiliacs and lack one of the clotting factors in their blood. If a short abalone is gashed by an ab iron and returned to the reef it will bleed to death. Divers should be careful not to cut abalone while removing them.

New divers are always looking for the abalone "hot spots." The truth is that abalone are very plentiful in Northern California. If you can free-dive to 40 feet you will have absolutely no trouble getting your limit of abalone off the beach at any of the most popular Nor Cal beaches. If you can only free-dive to 10 feet you'll have to think about where you dive a little more. All of the popular dive spots in Sonoma/Mendocino Counties yield a healthy crop of abs each year. However, years of diving pressure have taken their toll on abalone that are just off the beach and in shallow water. New divers should try to concentrate their diving in shallow water just north or south of the popular coves or swim up or down the coast as far as their endurance and skill will permit. If you have assess to a boat, dive kayak, or private access to seldom-dived areas you are in luck. In remote areas abalone may still be found in abundance in very shallow water.

So what do you do if you can only free-dive to 10 to 15 feet and have no boat or kayak? What should you do? My first suggestion would be to get a pair of fins into a pool and work on your physical condition and breath-hold capacity. Otherwise, newcomers to ab diving should avoid looking along the tops of rocks; the guy before you has already pulled those abs. Try looking at the base of rocks and in cracks. Abalone are often found upside down, back in the deepest cracks on the reef. They are often found looking like buttons as they cling

Free-Diver Catches World Record Abalone

In 1993 John Pepper, a general contractor from Half Moon Bay, caught the world's largest abalone. Among California sport divers this enormous abalone is nothing short of the Holy Grail.

Red abalone *(Haliotis rufescens)* must be a minimum of seven inches across to be legally taken and nine-inch animals are considered large. Catching an 11-inch animal is considered a once-in-a-lifetime experience. A 12-inch shell was unheard of until recently.

Pepper began his search for the world's largest abalone some 20 years ago. He liked abalone diving but only sought out large, trophy-sized animals. His search took him over most of the state of California and into Oregon. During this time he pulled 133 abalone over 10 inches, and 5 of those were over 11 inches.

Pepper had been diving for about two hours on September 5th "somewhere off the coast of Humboldt County." He is unwilling to describe the exact location. "Let's just say it's not easy to get to," he jokes. "You don't find as many abalone here as you do farther south, but the ones you do find are usually big," Pepper said.

As the light began to fade in the late afternoon, he stumbled on a large crack in only 12 feet of water, with an 11-inch abalone guarding the entrance. "Only after removing the first abalone and shinning my dive light back into the crack did I see the really big one," he described.

Pepper realized that this abalone was especially big, and he took almost two hours to pry the abalone from the rock. "When I first got my iron under the abalone and started to pry I could see the shell begin to crack." Not wanting to break his prize, he had to work the abalone iron in a little at a time during multiple free dives.

Pepper's abalone was 12 5/16 inches across, was 9 3/4 inches wide and weighed 11 3/5 pounds. This is both a world record and a state of California record. The male abalone had nice clean shell, free of parasites, unlike many other trophy abalone taken. The previous record was held by Don Thorp with an 11 3/4 inch abalone caught in 1983.

The abalone has been donated to a group of scientists for study. "It makes a lot more sense than eating it," Pepper said. However, he plans on keeping the shell. "It'd take a awful lot of money to get me to part with it," he said.

Some divers believe that this abalone may be very old. However, Konstantin Karpov, an Associate Marine Biologist with the California Department of Fish and Game refused to speculate on the age of the animal. "An abalone's growth rate may double from one year to the next," he says.

Karpov went on to say that, "It is impossible to say how large an abalone can get but that a 13-inch abalone is possible. Records are made to be broken." "Gigantism is common in most species and is epitomized by Pepper's shell," Karpov said. "This is a good time to look for trophy abalone due to the rapid growth observed lately," Karpov added.

Record-holder John Pepper shows his world record 12 5/16" abalone compared to a 7" abalone.

to a rocky reef just above a sandy area. There is often a thick layer of palm kelp growing just off the bottom in springtime. Try parting the kelp to find the abs underneath.

When you spot an ab, try to gauge it to see if it is legal. Instead of immediately attacking the ab with your iron, try grabbing on to a rock or a piece of kelp. This has two effects: first, it calms you so your breath lasts longer. Second, it allows you time to study how the ab is sitting on the rock and to determine the best place to insert your iron. If possible, you should measure the abalone prior to attempting to remove it.

The abalone iron is inserted between the food of the ab and the rock and rotated outward, all in one smooth motion. You are not "prying" the ab off the rock, but rather breaking the suction. Measure your ab and if it is undersized, put it back where you found it, or at least in a protected crack where it has time to suck down on a rock. An abalone thrown overboard will sit on the bottom, shell down, and die. They cannot turn themselves over.

Rock Scallops

We all know of the great bounty of seafood that the ocean gives up to divers. Some game may be difficult to bag because they either swim away or are difficult to find. However, one of the better tasting game animals in the sea just happens to be the easiest of all to catch.

Rock scallops *(Hinnites giganteus)* begin life as planktonic larva drifting at the mercy of the currents. As they grow larger they begin to lay down a hard shell and sink to the bottom, hopefully in a suitable habitat. At this time in their life, rock scallops look much like bay scallops with the common "Shell Oil Company" logo shape. They move around by jet propulsion by flapping their shells together.

Once they grow to about an inch or so in diameter, they then flap their way up into a rocky nook and begin to cement one shell to the rock. This is accomplished by extending their mantle and laying down shell material between their shell and the surrounding rock. When this material hardens they are stuck for good. Sedentary scallops grow very slowly and may take 25 years to reach 7 to 10 inches.

Rock scallop are normally found on offshore pinnacles that are subjected to strong currents. They are almost always found out of direct sunlight and normally have a covering of marine growth that makes them blend in with the surrounding rock.

A free-diver rises to the surface with an abalone catch.

A gray-mantle scallop lies hidden among corynactis anemones.

Scallops have many small eyes, each complete with a lens, cornea, and retina. The eyes are very sensitive to changes in light levels and can detect a diver from many feet away. Once a predator is detected it will then rapidly close, and this movement is often what draws your attention to the scallop. If you are a bit farther away when they close you may miss seeing the scallop altogether.

They are also sensitive to vibration, so divers who swim off the reef will see more "smiles." They may also be recognized by their bright red or green mantle. It is not known what causes this color difference, but most divers agree that the red ones taste better.

There are two ways to harvest scallops. The most common way is to take the entire animal. First, tap the shell with your dive knife or abalone iron. This causes the shell to close tighter and gives the shell more structural rigidity. If the scallop is sticking out from the rock, a blow from your hand or butt of your ab iron will dislodge the shell. Otherwise, place your ab iron under an exposed lip of the shell and pry. They normally pop off on the first try, but some require a little coaxing.

Another way to harvest scallops is to clean them underwater. Slip a thin, dull knife (such as a butter knife) between the shell halves and scrape (not cut) the muscle from the flatter of the two halves. That opens the shell and the muscle (or button) is easily scrapped from the other shell. A zip-lock plastic bag is the ideal way to get your catch to the surface. Be careful not to cut your button in half; the warden will count it as two scallops!

If you have harvested the entire animal you still have to clean it. Sometimes this is difficult since they close up tight and lack an opening to insert a knife. Try tickling them open by inserting a long thin object in the small gap between the shells at the hinge. A piece of eel grass is ideal. Gently stick your eel grass into the shell and move it around a bit. The shell will open enough for you to insert your knife and separate the muscle from the shell. All of the soft parts of the animal are edible, but most divers eat only the muscle and discard the rest. The organ meat should not be eaten if there is a risk of a red tide (May through November), and scallops should not be eaten from areas at risk from pollution. Call the State of California Pesticide and Environmental Toxicology Section at 510-540-3063 for more information on shellfish poisoning.

It is easier to get all of the meat out, and out in one piece, if you clean them topside. The scallop will stay fresher, longer if you leave it in the shell, and you will not have to argue with Fish and Game on the limit. Some like to clean and show off the shells as well.

However, the scallop has acquired seven years or more of marine growth and it seems a shame to remove it from the ocean. Cleaning the scallop on the boat and throwing the shell back into the ocean helps a bit, but the animals rarely drop onto a suitable habitat. It's also easier to swim back to the boat with ten buttons compared with 10 large shells.

The big decision is how to prepare your catch. Many like their scallops raw, right out of the shell.

That seems a little, shall we say, unrefined and many like their scallops either with a little lemon juice or, better yet, with wasabi (Japanese horseradish) and soy sauce.

If you insist on cooking them, be sure to cook them only a little, since they are easily overcooked and dried out. Try barbecuing them on a shish kebab or beer-battered and deep fried (Just add beer instead of water in any batter recipe). Anyway you prepare them, scallops are the most tender and sweetest meat that the ocean gives up to divers.

Sea Urchins

In an Italian market you might find them called Frutta di la mare or "fruit of the sea." Japanese call them uni, and consume millions of pounds each year. Some divers call them pin cushions, or some other unmentionable name when they place their hand on one. Most, however, simply call them urchins.

The sea urchin is a member of the echinoderm order and is related to sea stars, sea cucumbers, and sand dollars. Many do not consider them to be edible, and think of them as something to be smashed up for fish food. In some parts of the world urchins are toxic and should not be eaten. How-

Purple sea urchin.

ever, in California there are two species that are not only edible but are considered choice. The red urchin (*Strongylocentrotus franciscanus*) is considered the best of the California urchins. Over fifty million pounds were taken from California waters in 1988 alone and about 85 percent of that was exported to Japan. The somewhat less desirable purple urchin *(S. Purpuratus)* is also exported, but in smaller amounts.

To catch urchins you will need a knife or abalone iron to pry them from the rock, thick gloves, and a bag to carry your catch. Urchins are easy to catch. Simply pry them off their rock, pop them in your bag and off you go. Urchins may be found all along California's North Coast.

Once back on the beach you need to clean and prepare your catch. The only edible part of the urchin are the gonads or roe. Luckily, other than the shell the roe is the heaviest part of the urchin. Cut a hole or "test" around the mouth on the underside of the urchin. Drain out the fluid, and run your finger along the inside of the shell to dislodge the row. Pour the roe out and rinse, but do not soak, in cold, fresh water.

Urchin roe can vary from cream-colored to yellow to orange. The lighter the color the milder the flavor. The roe has a creamy, almost sweet flavor. Urchin may be eaten raw with a little wasabi and soy sauce, or on French bread with a little lemon juice. Alternatively, it may be quickly sauteed with a little butter. Bon appétit!

Lingcod

Lingcod are one of the most sought after fish by California divers. They may be found along the entire state and some ten million pounds are harvested annually. About six percent of the sport harvest is taken by spearfishers. Lingcod are one of the most commonly speared fish in California, second only to combined species of rockfish, genus Sebastes.

The scientific name for lings is *Ophiodon elongatus* meaning "snake tooth," and they are the largest member of the greenling, the Hexagrammidae, family. They should not be confused with unrelated Atlantic cod. Lingcod feed on juvenile rockfish, squid and their favorite food appears to be octopus. They lie in wait for an unsuspecting prey to wander too close, then pounce and grab their dinner with razor sharp teeth.

Lingcod are very territorial and most fish, par-

Lingcod.

ticularly the males, move around very little. During most of the year there is a segregation of sexes. The smaller males are found in shallow water less than 100 feet deep, while the females are found in water exceeding 100 feet and often to 400 feet. Because of this depth segregation some 70 percent of all lings taken by divers are males.

This situation changes in November through March when the females move inshore to breed. Eggs are laid in small caves or rocky depressions in 10 to 40 feet of water and are externally fertilized. Soon afterwards the female splits and leaves the male with the role of guardian. Lings are polygamists and a single male may guard as many as four nests during the seven-week incubation period. This house-husband will aggressively protect the egg mass from predators, such as crabs, and rockfish. Should the male be taken, the eggs will be rapidly consumed by other fishes. Most divers consider it very unsportsmanlike to shoot a nesting fish. Each nest contains some 500,000 eggs, and shooting the male will compromise the catch in the future.

When hunting lings look in small holes and for perches on top of rocky outcroppings. Have a little patience and look carefully since the fish blend in well to their surroundings. Sometimes a flashlight is helpful to find lings back in holes. Some divers attach the flashlight directly on to the end of their speargun. Should you startle a ling before you get off a shot, stick around the area. Lings are territorial and will usually return to their favorite perch rather quickly after being disturbed.

Some spearfishers have developed clever ways to attract lings. One technique is to take the butt of your dive knife and bang it on a rock several times. If there is a ling in a nearby hole, chances are he will come out to investigate all the clatter.

Another technique was developed by a friend of mine who would always take his wife diving and ask her to carry the stringer. Once a fish was speared he would regularly circle around behind her. Often he would find a big ling stalking his wife! Throughout the dive, each fish speared seemed to be bigger than the one before, and limits were often taken by this method. This practice is not recommended around sharks or marine mammals.

A heavy, two-banded speargun is suggested for taking big lingcod that can get up to 40 pounds or more. In the summer months when the smaller fish are inshore, a pole spear or a lighter gun will do. It is unwise to shoot a big fish with a pole spear or small rock gun.

Lingcod occasionally have a light green or blue color to their fillets. This color is due to their diet and in no way indicates that the fish is bad. In fact, the color always disappears on cooking. Try beer-battered ling or ling poached in wine sauce.

Rockfish

Rockfish, grouped into the genus Sebastes, are an important member of the reef community, and are the single largest fishery in California. Although the numbers vary a bit from year to year, on average they represent around 80 percent of the party boat catch (by numbers of fish) each year. Rockfish are good eating with large, firm flakes and a mild flavor.

Rockfish bear their young live and are just under a quarter inch when they are released into the water. At that time they are planktonic and drift with the currents for several months. They then concentrate near-shore and seek shelter in rocky areas and kelp beds. After one year they may grow to about 6 inches and then take another 15 years to reach 15 inches. Fish larger than 20 inches may be quite old.

Although quite similar in appearance, each species has developed different behavior characteristics and food preferences. For instance blue rockfish (*S. Mystinus*) are mostly found swimming in open water near kelp beds. Blues are opportunistic feeders and will eat whatever drifts past them. They are particularly fond of jellyfish, crustaceans and tunicates.

At the same time gopher rockfish (*S. carnatus*) prefer to inhabit the bottom around rocky areas and principally feed on crabs and shrimp. Kelp rockfish (*S. atrovirens*) will feed on planktonic creatures and do not swim very far from the kelp canopy.

Kelp rockfish.

Vermilion rockfish.

Rockfish are generally less than two feet long and will normally let you get fairly close to them. Some species, such as the vermilion *(S. miniatus)*, are quite shy so your stealth technique will have to be better for this colorful fish than others. In general, you'll not need a long speargun with many bands. A short, one-or-two band gun or small pneumatic works well, and these are often referred to as "rock guns," because they are easy to maneuver around rocky bottoms. Many prefer a pole spear or sling because they're quickly reloaded. Once you're in a school of fish, a speedy reload will often make the difference between landing one fish or many. A paralyzer head or a trident head works well for these small fish. Choose a robust head since you'll surely hit a rock if you miss your target.

Rockfish are often found in kelp beds along the entire California Coast. Areas near easy and popular entries are often sparse for fish, so you'll need to venture out where there are fewer divers. A kayak or boat helps.

California Halibut

While scientists use the Latin name *Paralichthys californicus*, divers refer to these enormous fish as "hallies" or "flaties," or the really big ones as "barn doors." No matter what you call them, the California halibut is one of the most sought after game fish by California spearfishers, and with good reason. It is the largest of the commonly speared fish and can grow up to be 5 feet long and weigh over 70 pounds. Fish in the 40-to 50- pound range are regularly taken by spearfishers. They are also one of the most challenging fish to locate and bag. Their camouflaged pattern blends in very well with their sandy bottom habitat and many divers, both novice and expert alike, swim over many fish without ever noticing. Once a large fish is speared, the real challenge is subduing the fish and getting it back to the beach or boat.

California halibut range along the western United States from Washington State to Baja, and are found on mud and sand bottoms from the surf line to well over 600 feet. They may be identified by their rather large mouth. Both eyes are usually, but not always, on the left side of the head, and the maxillary (upper jaw bone) extends past the eye. During the fall and winter, halibut feed in deep water on squid, anchovies and queenfish. Beginning about February the fish move inshore to depths of 60 feet or less for spawning, which lasts through July.

Newly hatched halibut are pelagic and drift at the mercy of the currents. At this stage the young fish appear much like other fish—they have an eye on

A diver shows off his catch of rockfish and lingcod.

Copper rockfish.

China rockfish.

each side of their head. During the next 20 to 30 days the fish begin to change. The right eye slowly migrates to the left side of the head, and the right, eyeless side becomes pale as the eyed side takes on the halibut's characteristic, camouflaged pattern. Occasionally, nature makes a mistake and the left eye is the one that migrates, or either a camouflaged pattern or the pale coloration develops on both sides. When the fish reach about 10 millimeters in length, they abandon their pelagic life and migrate into shallow bays and estuaries.

After the spawning season the adult fish remain in shallow water and June through September is the most productive time for spearfishers to seek these fish. During this time they are found from the surf zone down to 60 feet. In Northern California the height of the halibut season is June through August.

Divers should swim as far off the bottom as the visibility permits and look for the pattern of the fish on the sand bottom. Initially, the challenging part is recognizing the fish as you swim over it. Often the fish will bury itself under a thin layer of sand with only their eyes exposed, while at other times they will be found lying in plain view. Their camouflaged coloration makes them difficult to distinguish from the sand bottom. Learn to be able to pick the "halibut shaped" pattern out of the patterns of ripples in the sand. Where one fish is found there are usually more nearby.

Divers subdue a halibut.

Diving into History

Eighty years of seagoing activity saw thousands of cargoes moving up and down the coast. Of course the sea claimed its percentage and many a ship, cargo, and crew ended up in a watery grave. There was no reason for large amounts of gold or silver to be transported up the redwood coast since they were much safer in a bank back in San Francisco. Yet one man's debris is another man's treasure. The rich history of California's North Coast bay would more explored by divers if they know where and how to look.

Divers and the old dog-holers look for the same thing, a sheltered cove for safe access to the sea. The dog holes of yesteryear are today's dive sites. Divers looking for a bit of history often begin by noticing remains on shore and following them into the water. While the heaviest and least interesting artifacts are often found on shore, a horde of interesting artifacts, some of historical significance, can be found in underwater.

As in any port, things were often dropped in the water. Maybe a businessman or sailor dropped some personal item while traversing from ship to shore by high wire. As accidents always happen, we can only guess how much of the ships cargo was lost during the loading and unloading process.

Most frequently the port facilities were located at the north side of the dog hole coves. Ports with chutes or high wires had iron eye bolts sunk into solid rock. Many of these eye bolts still remain in place. The donkey engines and other large pieces of equipment were set on heavy, redwood timbers. While the engines have been removed a long time ago, the larger timbers still remain, a testament to the longevity of redwood.

Once these pieces of equipment are located, it is easy to imagine where a 100-foot schooner could have been tied and loaded. Old photographs or port records will give you additional insight on how ships anchored and where artifacts may be found underwater. A chute or cable was secured on the ocean floor offshore of the landing. In the early days a large anchor was used to secure the end of the chute and later concrete structures were used to secure wires. Many of the anchors that divers find in these ports were not lost from ships, but deliberately placed there. Often additional anchors would be used to securely fix the ship under the wire or chute.

Ports with wharves, for example Albion, had massive redwood timbers driven into the beach and sea floor. Even after 70 or more years many of these timbers are visible, particularly at low tide.

Of course a great many ships were lost in these ports

Loading by chute at Mendocino. Photo courtesy Mendoncino Historical Reasearch Inc.

and their artifacts are continually being found by divers. A few ships were lost when the captain misguided his ship and struck a submerged rock. Most of the captains were seasoned skippers and that did not happen very often.

The more likely cause of sinking is misjudging the weather. Schooners at anchor were quite vulnerable to a change in wind direction. Ports that were well sheltered from the northwesterly swell became raging cauldrons when a southerly storm blew through. Before steam engines became commonplace, the captain had to wait out the storm and hope the anchor did not drag. All too often the ship was smashed on the rocks directly below the loading facilities.

While divers occasionally find artifacts by luck, the more knowledgeable the diver, the more they are likely to find. The search for any wreck should first begin in a library. This is the antithesis of a romantic search, but only thorough tedious research are you likely to find a yet undiscovered wreck. It is often said of scientific research and is more true of researching shipwrecks that "an hour in the library will save you a month in the field."

There are several good libraries with extensive holdings from 19th century California. The Kelly House Museum in Mendocino is a good place to research North Coast History. My favorite place to begin my library search is the San Francisco Maritime Museum at Fort Mason. Besides having an extensive collection of old books, they have older editions of Loyds Register and a card catalog that lists California ships alphabetically. Entries in the catalog will refer readers to books that mention the ship as well as newspaper articles. The San Francisco Public Library has an extensive collection of old newspapers such as the *San Francisco Call*, *Examiner* and *Chronicle*. It is unfortunate that many of the shipping records were lost during the 1906 earthquake, but much still remains.

There are basically two ways to find a wreck: you

Dog-hole Ports

Mendocino County

Bear Harbor still goes by the same name. Mill began operation in 1891 and was shut down in 1899 when a tidal wave took out the wharf and chute.

Wolf Creek Timber operated a mill from 1949 to 1960 near the mouth of **Jackass Creek**. The mill was closed after a storm took out most of the buildings. There was never a landing since lumber was trucked inland, but artifacts remain.

Northport Landing was also called **Usal**. This was once the busiest ports in the area and loaded ships by wire chutes. Numerous mills were built and subsequently burned from 1890 to 1902. The port was located at the campground at the southern end of the Sinkyone Wilderness State Park.

Monroe Landing was also known as **Hales Grove Landing**. No access from shore except through private property.

Miller's Landing also went by **Cottanevas** and was located at the town of Rockport. Ships were loaded by slide and wire chutes. Various mills operated from 1880's to 1943. This was the location of the first steel suspension bridge on the west coast.

Hardy Creek Landing was located at the mouth of present-day Hardy Creek. A mill was first built and the 1896 and mills operated through 1911. This dog-hole had a 590-foot wharf and a wire chute.

Juan's Creek Landing was also called **Union Landing** and **Alviso Creek**, and was located at the mouth of present-day Juan's Creek. Lumbering began in early 1890s and operated through the 1940s. This is the site of a public beach.

Westport was once known as **Beall's** and later **Helmke's Landing**. The port had two wharves, two slides and a wire chute, and operated from 1852 through the 1950s. Remains may be found out shore from Cobweb Palace Hotel. Many ships sunk here.

Switzer's Chute used a slide chute. The dog-hole was located at **Bruhel Point** near MEN 74.54.

Kibesillah Landing was a busy place in the late 1800s. Ships were loaded via slide chute and a wharf. This dog-hole was located near MEN 73.58. This is near the site of the Pacific Star Winery.

Ackman's Landing was also called **Newport** and had a slide chute. This abandoned town is now the site of a ranch one mile south of Kibesillah near MEN 72.32.

Laguna Landing, now called **Cleone**, and is in the northern part of MacKerricher State Park. This north-facing cove was a good winter anchorage and had both a wharf and slide chutes. Mills operated from the late 1880's to the 1950's.

Fort Bragg had a wharf on north side of the cove, and three schooners wrecked here. Mills began operation in 1885, and Georgia Pacific Lumber Company continues to operate a mill at this site. It is the only operational mill on this part of the coast.

Noyo Landing is located at present day Noyo Cove. The site had wire and slide chutes, eight wrecks here. Mills operated beginning in 1858.

Pallas Bay at Hare Creek had a slide chute.

Bromley Landing at Mitchell Creek has a slide chute.

Caspar Landing had two slide chutes, a wire, and a wharf. Six ships were wrecked here. Mill operated from 1880 through the 1950s.

Russian Gulch, now Russian Gulch State Park, had two slide chutes a wire, and a wharf. Two ships wrecked here. Mills operated from 1888 through the 1920s.

Mendocino Landings were located north of Big River. Henry Mieggs built the first mill on the bluffs south of town in 1852, and later moved it to the flats next to **Big River**. Two chutes and two wires were strung from bluffs near the town, and there were at least 12 wrecks here. Lumbering was a off and on through the 1950s.

Little River, now part of Van Damme State Park, had a wharf and slide chutes. Five ships were wrecked here. Lumbering began in 1864, and 14 schooners were built on this beach.

Big Gulch, also called **Pullen's Landing**, had a slide chute, and is now called **Buckhorn Cove**. Mill operated from 1878 to 1910.

Albion had a lumber mill and wharf on north bank. Four ships were wrecked here, and anchors are found in the outer cove. Also, a slide chute (Handley's Chute) was located on the south side of Albion Cove. This was the site of Mendocino County's first mill in 1852.

Salmon Creek Landing, was also called **Whitesboro Cove** and was located at mouth of Salmon Creek just south of Albion Cove. Originally lumber was shipped by rail to Albion. In 1880 a mill and port were constructed. This dog-hole had a small wharf on the south side of the cove. Four ships were wrecked here.

Navarro Landing at the mouth of the Navarro River and was also called **Wendling**. The port had a wharf, and at least four ships were wrecked here. Mills operated beginning in 1851.

Cuffey's Cove was located at the mouth of Laurel Gulch and was located below the Cuffey's Cove Cemetery. This dog-hole had two slide chutes.

Greenwood Landing, the remains of a chute located west of the old Elk Post Office, a wire ran between the bluff and three offshore rocks. Much lumber and shipping activity occurred here over the years.

Uncle Abe's Landing was three-quarter mile south of Wharf Rock at Greenwood. A small slide chute operated her for a short time. The landing was on the south side of the south point of the cove at MEN 37.07.

New Haven was near the mouth of Irish Gulch and had a slide chute and a wire, two wrecks here.

Hoag' Landing, also called **Bridgeport Landing**, had two slide chutes and a wire, one ship was wrecked here. This dog-hole is located north of Mills Creek.

Arena Cove had a wharf, slide chutes and a wire. Mills began operation in 1869 and this site now has public wharf.

Buster's Landing, also called **France's Landing**, had a slide chute. The landing was on a bluff about halfway between Arena Cove and Scout's landing.

Scout's Landing had a slide chute. This dog-hole was located at the mouth of Moat Creek. The creek got its name form the moat-like structure at its mouth.

Saunder's Landing, also called **Hearn's Landing**, had a wire. This dog-hole was located at the mouth of Haern Gulch.

Iversen's Landing was also called **Rough and Ready**, and **Ferguson's Cove**. This dog-hole was located at the end of Iversen's Road, and had slide chutes and a wire; five schooners were lost here.

Hard Scratch Landing, also called **Steen's Landing**, was located at the mouth of Signal Port Creek. It had a slide chute, and one ship was wrecked here.

Nip-and-Tuck Landing had many names and was located at mouth of Roseman Creek. It had a slide chute, at least one shipwreck here.

Haven's Anchorage, was also known as **Fish Rocks Landing**. Access to the old landing is through Anchor Bay Campground. Many ships were lost here including *SS Crescent City*.

Collin's Landing, also called **St. Ores**, was located at the Mouth of Saint Ores Creek. This dog-hole has a slide cute and a wire.

Bourne's Landing, also known as **Bowen's Landing**, was located at the mouth of Bourne's Gulch. The port had two slide chutes and a wire; two ships wrecked here.

Robinson's Landing had one slide chute and a wire. This dog-hole is on the south side of Robinson Point, about one-half mile north of Gualala.

Sonoma County

Del Mar Landing is currently the site of the marine reserve at The Sea Ranch.

Joe Tonga's Landing was located at Stengel Beach, The Sea Ranch. This dog-hole had a steam driven winch and a swinging boom.

Bihler's Landing had two slide chutes from the north point of Pebble Beach, The Sea Ranch. Two dog-holers were wrecked here.

Black Point Landing was in the southern portion of The Sea Ranch.

Stewart's Point had three slide chutes, and a wire. Five ships were wrecked here.

Fisk Mill Cove, near the northern boundary of Salt Point State Park, had a slide chute.

Salt Point Cove, also called **Gerstle's Cove**, has two slide chutes. This cove was named after the tide pools where Indians would gather salt. *SS Norlina* wrecked in the little cove south of Gerstle's.

Walsh's Landing, now called Ocean Cove, had a chute from north bluff.

Stochhoff's Cove is now called **Stillwater Cove** and is a Sonoma County Regional Park. This was the site of a boy's school and the school "borrowed" the name "Still Water" when the dog-hole to the south closed. This was not a true "dog-hole" and no commercial logging went on here.

Still Water Cove had a slide chute. This is not the present day Stillwater Cove Regional Park, but two-thirds of a mile south of the park.

Timber Cove had two slide chutes and a wire; one wreck here.

Moss Landing had a slide chute. This dog-hole was on the north side of Northwest Cape, Fort Ross State Park.

Fort Ross Cove had a chute that extended east from the western point. Many wrecks here including *SS Pomona*.

Russian Gulch was called **Jenner Landing** and was located at the site of the present-day state park. It had a short, very steep chute on southeast point. The wreckage of the schooner *William Sparks* on is the beach here.

Rule's Landing had wire chute from the north side of a triangular cove, just south of Russian Gulch. John Rule built a sawmill on the south fork of Russian Gulch in 1875.

Jenner Village was located at the site of present-day Jenner. Mr. Davis built a mill here and shipped lumber up river by barge. All coastal shipments went over the wire at Jenner Landing (Russian Gulch).

Duncan's Landing was six miles north of Bodega Head. This beach is now maintained by Sonoma Coast State Beach system.

Bodega Bay was not a true dog-hole since it had a good anchorage. This was the site of a Russian trading post from 1809 to 1812.

can research the name of a specific ship, or the locations where wrecks are known to occur. Many ships were sunk at port while they were loading. Included is a list of the dog-hole ports in Northern California. Most of these old ports are popular dive sites today, and included are both the old and new names. Besides the information provided, here local divers are a good source of additional information. There is a good reference series, "The United States Coast Pilot, Pacific Coast" that was intended to guide captains into ports. They identify approaches to ports and give the location of the port facilities.

Of course many ships were sunk while traveling up and down the coast. The steam schooners practiced a risky habit known as "hogging the beach." To give their passengers a comfortable ride captains would steer as close as possible to the coast, avoiding much of the wind and swell. Back then they did not have satellite navigation and would plot a course by dead reckoning (presuming the ship was traveling in a straight line at a constant speed and guessing how far they had gone before turning to avoid a headland). If the wind or currents changed their speed significantly the ship often ended up on the rocks.

Because of this habit the south side of major headlands are a good place to find wrecks. Divers will find that the Coast Guard has conveniently marked the more likely spots with lighthouses. Later some of these were replaced with whistle buoys. Lighthouses were only erected after a compelling need was established, usually after several ships became wrecked. The conditions near lighthouses are not normally good for diving—strong currents, rough water, no shelter

from wind. However, on a calm day divers may enjoy searching near lighthouses or southeast of where the wreck likely occurred.

If you know the name of a vessel, it is a relatively simple matter to find the ship in the Loyds Register and learn something about its size and structure. In San Francisco Maritime Museum you can then use the card catalog to locate any book references, newspaper articles, or transcripts that will invariably follow after the sinking. These will give the general location of the wreck. However, much if the information is in error and the prudent treasure hunter will compare information from a variety of sources before making a single dive.

Ships and wreckage move around after sinking and you'll need to view the wreck site for additional clues to where the wreck sits today. The northwesterly wind would often pull the wreckage off the beach and deposit it in deeper water, or drive it to the nearest beach directly southeast of the original wreck site. Divers might want to begin their search for sunken dog-holers near the loading facilities, but the area southeast of the port should be searched as well.

There are many books that may be good places to begin to look for shipwrecks: *California Shipwrecks* by Don B. Marshall, *Encyclopedia of American Shipwrecks* by Bruce D. Berman, *A Guide to Sunken Ships in American Waters* by Adrian L. Lonsdale and H.R. Kaplan, *Sail & Steam on the Northern California Coast* by Wallace E. Martin, *Ships of the Redwood Coast* by Jack McNairn and Jerry MacMullen, *Shipwrecks of the Pacific Coast* by James A. Gibbs, Jr..

A diver with ab iron and abalone catch.

Diving Regulations
Game Hunting

A California Sport Fishing License is required to take game and a special abalone stamp and "report card" is now required. Sport divers are limited to 100 abalone per year. The license must be in your possession while diving. In your possession for the license means on the beach if you have no vessel, or otherwise on your boat or kayak. Fishing regulations change frequently, so it is advisable to check current regulations before attempting to take game. For up to date Fish and Game regulations visit "www.dfg.ca.gov/title/d1_c4_a1.html" on the web.

Abalone: The rules and regulations concerning the sport take of abalone are the most complex of any fishery. The complexity of these rules reflects the complexity of the life cycle of the abalone, as well as the ingenuity of sportsmen to find loop-holes in the laws. What follows is a brief description of rules regarding the take of abalone north of San Francisco (no abalone may be taken south of San Francisco).

North of San Francisco abalone may be taken by sport divers from April 1st through June 30th, and August 1st through November 31st. Commercial take of abalone in California is prohibited, and there is no sport take permitted south of San Francisco.

Scuba may **not** be used to take abalone; only breath-hold diving is allowed. Scuba or surface-supplied air devices are not allowed aboard any vessel used by divers for taking abalone. The diver must have a valid California fishing license with abalone stamp, as well as an abalone "report card." A legal ab iron (see fish and game regulations for specifics) and a fixed caliper measuring device must be in your possession in the water.

Northern California divers normally find only one species of abalone, the red abalone. Reds must be at least seven inches across the largest dimension. The possession and daily bag limit is four abalone. That means that you may take only four abalone per day, and when you have your limit you may not put one legal-sized ab back so that you may find a bigger one (upgrading). Taking your limit and that of another (dry sacking) is illegal. If you have abalone in your freezer, you may only take more until the total in your possession is four.

Abalone may not be possessed or transported out of the shell, except for preparation for immediate consumption. One ranger defines, "for immediate consumption" as "the fire should be hot." That means that you may not clean your catch before hitting the road home. Yes, cleaning and slicing your catch and putting it back in the shell can get you fined.

Free-divers prepare to enter the water at Russian Gulch.

Legal limit for red abalone is 4 per diver, per day.

Rock Scallops: The daily bag limit for scallops in California is 10. If you clean your catch, be careful not to cut the button in half. The Fish and Game warden will count your two half buttons as two whole scallops! There is no closed season, nor is there a minimum size limit. Scuba is permitted to take scallops.

Sea Urchins: Divers may take 35 urchins per day, and there is no closed season or size limit. Scuba is permitted to take urchins.

Fin fish: Regulations on fin fish have become increasingly complex and species specific. Halibut, rockfish, lingcod, and more all have varying bag limits, size limits, and seasons depending on specifically where you will be spearfishing. Consult the current fish and game regulations for the specific species you wish to hunt and for the area you want to dive.

In general, no more than 20 fin fish in combination of all species with not more than 10 of any one species, may be taken or possessed by any one person except as otherwise provided. Within the overall bag limit of 20 fish, the following special limits apply:

Lingcod

Open season all year except during the months March and April in waters from Lopez Point, Monterey County, north to Cape Mendocino, Humboldt County. Limit is 2 with a minimum length of 26 inches total length. Lingcod fillets must be a minimum of 18 inches in length. Each fillet shall bear intact a one-inch square patch of skin.

Rockfish (Sebastes)

Open season all year except during the months of March and April in waters from Lopez Point, Monterey County, north to Cape Mendocino, Humboldt County. Limit is 10 in any combination of species, except that only 3 fish may be bocaccio, and 3 may be canary rockfish.

There is no size limit, except for bocaccio, minimum 10 inches. Rockfish: fillets must have the entire skin attached. Brown-skinned rockfish fillets shall be a minimum of 6 1/2 inches in length. Boccacio fillets must be a minimum of 5 inches in length.

Additional Fish:

California Halibut: Limit of 3 on the North Coast with a minimum size of 22 inches total length.

Cabezon: Limit of 10 and a minimum size of 14 inches total length.

Kelp Greenling & Rock Greenling: Limit of 10 with minimum size of 12 inches total length.

California Scorpionfish (Sculpin): Limit of 10 with minimum size of 10 total inches.

Marine Reserves

Point Cabrillo Reserve, Mendocino County. No form of marine life may be taken from the ocean area within 1,000 feet of the high tide mark in the vicinity of Point Cabrillo U.S. Coast Guard Lighthouse, bounded by lines extending due west (magnetic) 2,500 feet north and 1,600 south of the lighthouse. Access is free but a permit is required, call 707-937-5804.

Del Mar Landing Ecological Reserve, The Sea Ranch, Sonoma County. Fishing is permitted for fin fish only; no invertebrates may be taken. Spearguns may be used for the taking of fin fish. Swimming, boating, skin and scuba diving are permitted. The reserve extends seaward 1,000 feet from the high tide mark and extends for .59 of a mile from a bit north of Del Mar Point, southward. If you are north of the turn-around at the end of Helm Street and south of the turn-around at the end of Sounding Street you are outside of the reserve.

Gerstle Cove, Sonoma County. No form of marine life may be taken within 600 feet of the high water line in the most northerly portion of Gerstle Cove. The reserve is marked by posts on the bluff above the cove.

Bodega Marine Life Refuge, Marin County. No invertebrate or plant life may be taken. Taking of fin fish is permitted. This refuge is bounded by the mean high tide mark seaward for 1,000 feet, and between the northern boundary extended northwesterly and the southern boundary extended southwesterly of the Bodega Bay Marine Laboratory.

Cabezon.

Gerstle Cove, Salt Point State Park.

Point Reyes Headlands Reserve, Marin County. No form of marine life may be taken from the ocean area within 1,000 feet of the high tide mark in the Pt. Reyes Headlands, bounded on the west by a line extending due west (true) from Pt. Reyes Lighthouse and on the east by a line extending due east (true) from Chimney Rock.

Estero de Limantour Reserve, Marin County. No form of marine life may be taken below the high water mark in Estero de Limantour. Estero de Limantour includes all tideland waters to high water mark in an easterly direction from a line drawn north (true) from the extreme westerly point of Limantour Spit.

Duxbury Reef Reserve, Marin County. No game except abalone, dungeness crabs, rock crabs, rockfish, lingcod, cabezon, surfperch, halibut, flounder, sole, turbot, salmon, kelp greenling, striped bass, steelhead, monkeyface-eel, wolf-eel, smelt and silversides may be taken between the high tide mark and 1,000 feet beyond the low tide mark, between the westerly extension of the southerly boundary of the Pt. Reyes National Seashore and the southerly extension of the centerline of Kale Road in Bolinas Beach.

Farallon Islands Ecological Reserve, San Francisco County. This ecological reserve extends one nautical mile from the coastline of Southeast Farallon and North Farallon Islands. No one may go ashore on any of the Farallon Islands without a permit. Boating, sport and commercial fishing, swimming, and skin and scuba diving are permitted. All vessels shall observe a five nautical mile per hour speed limit within 1,000 feet of any shoreline in the reserve.

From March 15 through August 15 of each year, no vessel shall be operated or anchored less than 300 feet from the shoreline of any of the four islets comprising the North Farallons, including North Farallon, the Island of St. James and the two unnamed islets located between them, except in the area beginning at a line extending due west magnetic from the northernmost point of land on North Farallon and continuing clockwise to a line drawn due west magnetic from the southernmost point of land on North Farallon and in the area beginning at a line drawn due west magnetic from the northernmost point of land on the northernmost of the two unnamed islets and extending clockwise to a line drawn due south magnetic from the southernmost point of land on that islet.

From March 15 through August 15 of each year, no vessel shall be operated or anchored less than 300 feet from the shoreline in the area beginning at the south end of Jordan Channel, westward around Indian Head, then generally northward past Great Arch Rock, then generally following the shoreline to a line extending due west from the northernmost point of land on Sugarloaf Island or in the northeasternmost point of land on Saddle Rock (Seal Rock) then generally southwest along the northerly shoreline of Saddle Rock to the southwesternmost point of land on Saddle Rock and continuing generally northward to the west end of Mussel Flat. Both areas are at Southeast Farallon Island. Nothing in this section shall prohibit emergency anchorage or vessel operation necessary to protect property or human life.

Gulf of the Farallones and Cordell Bank National Marine Sanctuaries. These National Marine Sanctuaries encompass the waters around the Farallon Islands and the Cordell Bank and are continuous with the Monterey Bay National Marine Sanctuary to the south. Contrary to the name, the sanctuaries do not regulate either sport of commercial fishing. They do prohibit mining the sea floor and drilling for oil, prohibits certain kinds of ocean dumping, and makes stronger other existing laws to protect marine mammals, birds, and turtles. For additional information, sanctuary boundaries, and a complete text of the rules, contact the Sanctuary office at 415-556-3509; or on the web at "www.sanctuaries.nos.noaa.gov".

Artifact Hunting. The State of California claims ownership of all wrecks in offshore waters. It is illegal to remove artifacts from wrecks, particularly historic wrecks, without a permit. Contact the State for more information: California State Lands Commission, Submerged Cultural Resources Unit, 1807 13th Street, Sacramento, CA 95814, or call: 916-323-8487

Kathleen Apalatea shows a prize catch of red abalone.

Introduction to Mendocino County

Mendocino County boasts one of the most scenic and rugged coastlines in the world. Each year visitors marvel at sheer cliffs that drop hundreds of feet directly to emerald-green water below and a coastline sculptured by wind and waves into a maze of small bays, points, caves, and arches. Public access is sometimes limited due to the area's ruggedness and the abundance of private property. However, there are plenty of publicly accessible sites with excellent diving.

Mendocino County receives far less diver traffic each year than points south. This is not because of the lack of superb dive sites, for there are many, but rather because of the distance from San Francisco. It seems that most bay area divers are not willing to drive the extra hour to Mendocino, except, perhaps, on holiday weekends. Those who don't venture north of Sonoma County don't know what they're missing, since everything here exists on a much grander scale. This is the land where divers can find 10-inch red abalone, where lingcod grows to be 30, 40, or more pounds, and the vastness and scale of the reef itself outshines anything farther south. Just like Texas, everything seems bigger on the north coast.

The northern portion of Mendocino County is largely inaccessible from the shore. North of Westport, Highway 1 heads east and coastal access via good roads is not available until one reaches Eureka in Humboldt County. Most of this area is contained within the Sinkyone Wilderness, but locals simply refer to it as the "Lost Coast." There is limited access via dirt roads to this region, but most diving here is done via boats out of Shelter Cove. Here is where freedivers search for trophy abalone and fish.

Between the Lost Coast and the town of Fort Bragg is the sleepy little town of Westport and the Westport-Union Landing State Beach. This part of the coastline offers excellent shore diving on calm days, but the visibility here is not as good as the rest of Mendocino County. For the most part Westport is only visited local divers.

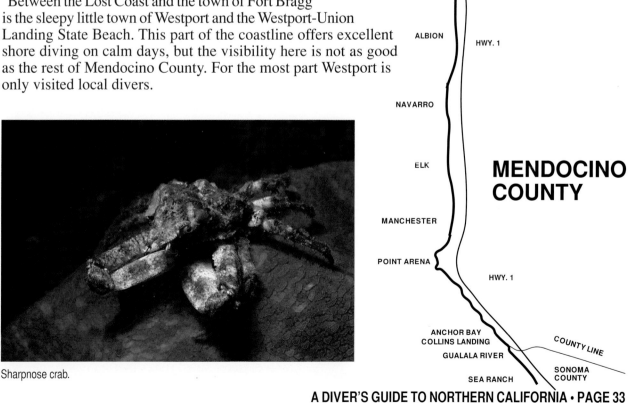

Sharpnose crab.

South of Fort Bragg to Navarro lies the heart of Mendocino diving. Here the coastline is rugged and rocky, and there are numerous and excellent sites to accommodate divers of all experience levels. Some are protected entries with easy access to sand beaches, and others are double black diamond entries that will thrill the most experienced diver. Sites accessible only from boats are pristine, colorful and full of game.

Between Navarro and Anchor Bay is largely a diver's wasteland with few public access points and a large stretch of sand known as Manchester Beach. There are two exceptions to this generalization. One is at Elk where there are a few public entries that athletic, advanced divers will enjoy. The other is at Point Arena where there is a good boat launch to explore offshore pinnacles, including the superlative diving at Arena Rock.

The coast a bit north of Anchor Bay has great diving but few public access points. If you want to dive here you can launch a boat out of Point Arena or Anchor Bay, or make friends with one of the land owners. Anchor Bay and Collins Landing are the most southerly Mendocino site covered in this book and should not be overlooked by coastal divers.

The southern end of the county is marked by the town of Gualala. There is not much diving here due to outfall from the Gualala River but how the town got its name is an interesting story. In the language of the Pomo "Wah-lah'-lay" meant "where the river meets the sea" and early European settlers used the name. When the town got big enough to have its own post office, an uninformed postal clerk presumed that the name derived from Spanish since the land was once part of a Mexican land grant and spelled the name of the post office "Gualala." This was a double error since the Mexicans really spelled it "Valale." Locals still use, and appreciate when others use, the original "Walalla." By the way, the scientific name for the flat abalone, *Haliotis Walallensis*, is named for this town.

In addition to tourism, and particularly diving tourism, the Mendocino coast supports a healthy economic base. The county has numerous communities grown up around fishing, lumbering, ranching and, recently, wine making. For each site I have included contact information for campgrounds and diver-friendly lodging. In addition to these there are county-wide brokers who will find you an up-scale rental for your diving trip: Try calling Shoreline Properties, 707-964-1444, or 800-WHAT-A-VU; Serenisea, 707-884-3836, 800-331-3836, or www.serenisea.com for more information.

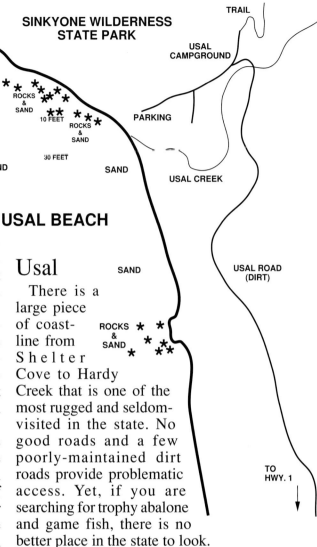

USAL BEACH

Usal

There is a large piece of coastline from Shelter Cove to Hardy Creek that is one of the most rugged and seldom-visited in the state. No good roads and a few poorly-maintained dirt roads provide problematic access. Yet, if you are searching for trophy abalone and game fish, there is no better place in the state to look.

Numerous lumber mills sprang up along this part of the coast from about 1880 through the early 20th Century. Bear Harbor, Needle Rock, Jackass Creek, and Usal all had fairly sizable towns. At Usal Mr. Wonderley built a mill in 1889, and a larger-than-average settlement sprang up around it. After Wonderley's death the mill and landing were run by a Scotsman, Robert Dollar. Dollar had to re-build his wharf every year and bought his own schooner, the *Newsboy*, to transport lumber to San Francisco. Mills operated off and on through depressions and boom times until 1902 when the Usal Redwood Company closed down for good.

Conditions on the Lost Coast are rarely pretty, and often quite rough as the area has no protection from wind and swell. This is an area to hunt for trophy abalone. Launch your boat or kayak from Shelter Cove, Usal or Bear Harbor and explore offshore rocks and islands.

The bottom in this area consists of sand with massive, steep-sided rocks that jut out of the sand like steel girders. These rocks are covered with palm and other short-stalked kelp, and there is a noticeable lack of bull and giant kelp. Abalone here are more sparse than points south, but they are much bigger. Ten-inchers are common, but it will take a bit of hunting to find an abalone over eleven or—if lady luck is with you—over twelve inches. Marine life in this area is not as pretty as points south.

When you clean abalone from this area, look for abalone pearls in the meat and reproductive gland. Abalone caught near sandy bottoms often incorporate sand into their tissues. The abalone covers the grain of sand with layers upon layers of shell material. After many years have passed the sand grain develops into a fine pearl.

Access, Entry, and Hazards: Boats may be launched from Shelter Cove. This is a long drive on Briceland Road and Shelter Cove Road west from Garberville. You may also launch a small boat or kayak from Usal. From Highway 1, at MEN 90.88 take County Road 431 north. The dirt road winds through a pine and fir forest with some spectacular views of the Lost Coast for six and one-half miles. The road eventually drops to a wide sandy beach with public camping. This is the southern end of the Sinkyone Wilderness State Park. Park in the lot on the north side of the Usal Creek. Kayaks and inflatable boats may be launched here to explore the pristine sites. The best ab diving is north of the beach among the numerous offshore rocks. Pit toilets and primitive camping is available for a fee. Bring your own water. The road is closed in winter.

Watch for big waves and surge along this entire stretch of coastline. Conditions can change rapidly, so be alert and cautious. White sharks have been seen here.

Westport-Union Landing

The five-mile stretch of coastline between Hardy Creek and Westport is one of most accessible in all of the county, and four miles of this area is within the boundaries of the Westport-Union Landing State Beach. Public access points have well-maintained stairways, toilets, and numerous camping areas.

This part of the coast enjoyed a busy history. Lloyd Beall settled the area in 1864, began cutting lumber and built a chute to load schooners at Westport. About the same time Alfred Wages settled at the mouth of the creek that now bears his name, and thus began nearly 100 years of lumbering. One of the first towns

in the area was at Kibesillah, about five miles south of Westport. Small towns sprang up at Newport, Westport, and Union Landing. The Rockport Redwood Company operated a mill here from 1938 to 1957 and was the last working mill in the area. Lumber first went out "under the wire" at Juan Creek, at that time called Union Landing, and then by truck.

This area is a home to plentiful and large abalone, and larger-than-average game fish, including lingcod, cabezon, and numerous species of rockfish. Offshore reefs are comprised of rock and sand that begins at the surf line and gently slopes down to over 60 feet. The invertebrate life here is not as colorful as points south, but you'll find nice patches of corynactis, tunicates, and rock scallops. Abalone near shore are numerous and shore picking can be good, particularly at Hardy

HWY. 1

HARDY CREEK

JUAN CREEK

UNION LANDING

WESTPORT-UNION LANDING
STATE BEACH

ABALONE POINT

DEHAVEN CREEK

WAGES CREEK

PETE'S BEACH

WESTPORT

BELL PT.

HWY. 1

Hardy Creek.

Creek. Once you reach depths of 20 feet or more, you'll find more and bigger abalone. This is a good area to chase 10-inch abalone. The sandy areas are good to look for abalone with pearls.

Access, Entry, and Hazards: There are numerous places to enter the water along this part of the coast. Watch for big waves and surge. White sharks sightings are common in this area. Call 707-964-4406 for state beach and camping information.

• **Hardy Creek** - Park at the turnout on the west side of Highway 1 at MEN 83.53. This is where Highway 1 heads east and leaves the coast. Take the short, but steep trail to the sandy beach. Cross the creek and head north to the offshore rocks. This is a good spot to launch kayaks, and for shore picking of abalone. There are no facilities.

• **Juan Creek** - Park at the north side of Juan Creek at MEN 82.91. Scamper over the rock wall to the wide sandy beach. This is another good spot to launch kayaks to explore offshore areas. There are no facilities.

• **Abalone Point** - Enter the State Beach at the De Haven Parking Area at MEN 79.30 from Highway 1. Proceed north about one-half mile and park in the small parking at the base of the prominent point. Take the staircase to the beach and swim to the rocks off the point. You may also enter at the staircase near the mouth of De Haven Creek. Pit toilets are located near the entry point and there is a camping for some distance between Highway 1 and the beach.

• **Wages Creek** - Enter the private campground at MEN 78.07. This is a good place to launch kayaks and small inflatables for access to great spearfishing and abalone hunting, especially trophy abalone. The campground has toilets and showers. Call 707-964-2964 for reservations.

• **Pete's Beach** - Park at the Pete's Beach Parking Area at MEN 77.76. Take the staircase to the beach and dive around the offshore rocks to the south. There are no facilities.

• **Westport** - There are several public access points within the town of Westport. One is on the south side of town at MEN 77.17. Turn west onto the Pacific Avenue Loop (County Road 426A) and park along the road near the ocean. Take the steep and dangerous trail to the beach. Another entry is near the center of Westport. Turn west on Omega Drive (County Road 428E) and park along the road near Highway 1. Take the steep, slippery, and dangerous trail to the gravel beach. Beware of raspberry thorns.

Lingcod.

Kibesillah

In the middle of the Nineteenth Century the Stewart Family left Illinois and moved first to Iowa then Washington State. An Indian uprising in the late 1850s caused them to move again. Some of the family ended up settling near Fisherman's Bay (Sonoma County) and left their name on the point between Salt Point State Park and The Sea Ranch.

Calvin Stewart spent some time with his older brother in Bridgeport and eventually sought his own fortune just north of the Ten Mile River. He called the landing and the town "Newport." This was located one-half mile north of South Kibesillah View Area. In the beginning Calvin had more than his share of trouble. His store burnt down while everyone was building the foundation for a slide chute. When the chute was finally built, a storm took the whole thing out and it had to be rebuilt. A landing was considered successful if a ship had to wait less than a week before the weather would allow it to pick up its load. By this standard the landing proved workable and Calvin was on his way.

Just north of Newport was the town of Kibesillah. It was called the "coming metropolis of the North Coast." With two hotels, a church, a school and two saloons, who could have thought otherwise. Kibesillah was first a trading post and a gathering place for the local ranchers and potato farmers. With Calvin's success at Newport, Kibesillah built a wharf of its own with a slide chute. The town, however, did not last long. When the nearby Abalobdiah Creek was logged out in 1885, the town began to dry up. Calvin and his partners set up a new mill at Fort Bragg, and by 1890 only a few ranchers were left.

Today divers find convenient access near the South Kibesillah View Area. Only a few metal supports and a brick wall remain from the dog hole days, probably all that is left of someone's house. However, the diving is excellent.

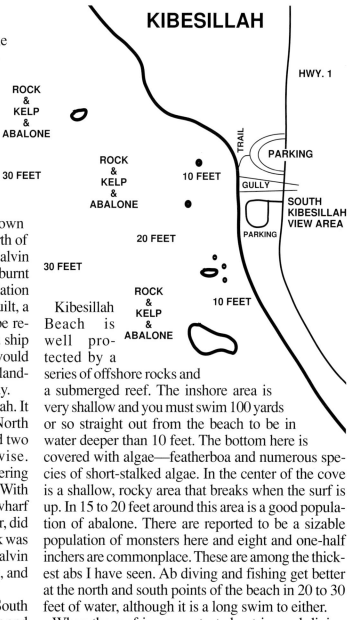

Kibesillah Beach is well protected by a series of offshore rocks and a submerged reef. The inshore area is very shallow and you must swim 100 yards or so straight out from the beach to be in water deeper than 10 feet. The bottom here is covered with algae—featherboa and numerous species of short-stalked algae. In the center of the cove is a shallow, rocky area that breaks when the surf is up. In 15 to 20 feet around this area is a good population of abalone. There are reported to be a sizable population of monsters here and eight and one-half inchers are commonplace. These are among the thickest abs I have seen. Ab diving and fishing get better at the north and south points of the beach in 20 to 30 feet of water, although it is a long swim to either.

When the surf is up, protected entries and diving may be found behind the large rocks at the south end of the beach. Locals claim that some really big aba-

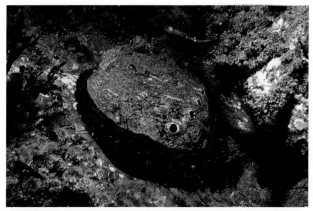

Red abalone.

Rainbow sea star.

lone are taken here each year. On my last outing I was only to find a few smallish, but legal, abalone here. This area is only in five to seven feet of water and I find this kind if diving in thick kelp to be tiring. I'd much rather hunt in 30 feet of water and not get tossed around so much.

Access, Entry, and Hazards: On Hwy. 1 park in the roundabout at MEN 71.95. This is on the north side of the South Kibesillah View Area. For reference the View Area (with no beach access) is on the south side of the gulch, and beach access on the north side. Follow the short, but very steep trail to the gravel beach. Locals have left a rope to aid your descent and ascent along the last part of the trail. Watch for big waves and surge. Offshore rocks and reef protect the cove fairly well from northwesterly waves. However, the cove is facing northwest, and when the northweserlies pick up this place can get ugly.

You may also find coastal access to good diving at North Mussel Rocks (MEN 74.54) and Mussel Rocks (MEN 74.09). At each turnout a one-quarter mile trail will take you to a rocky entry. The trail is gently slopping and there is a short scramble down a rocky cliff to the water. There is good abalone diving and tank diving if you can handle the hike.

MacKerricher State Park

Located just north of the town of Fort Bragg, MacKerricher State Park stretches for about three miles from Pudding Creek to just north of the town of Cleone. The southern part of the Park is characterized by a sandy beach with rolling beakers that is inhospitable to divers. However, along the northern portion of the Park is Laguna Point. This point not only provides shelter from the ocean swell but also the rocky substrate for a healthy reef community.

This Park was once the homestead site of the Scottish immigrant Duncan MacKerricher. He purchased the land in 1868 and deeded it to the state in 1949. The calm cove in the northern part of the park was once the site of a dog hole port where schooners

loaded lumber bound for San Francisco. That port was called Cleone, a name that now belongs to the small town just east of the park. The area did not have the large stands of lumber as other California dog holes and the port was dwarfed by nearby Fort Bragg.

Most of the artifacts from those bygone days have either rotted away or have been removed by the state. However, divers may find iron artifacts around the tip of Laguna Point. Several of the wash rocks at the point have large iron rings cemented to them. These rings were used to tie off schooners as their holds were being filled.

At the far tip of Laguna Point is an assortment of large, flat wash rocks. These are located just offshore and are home to a resident population of harbor seals. This is one of the better places in the state to view harbor seals. This is due, in part, because there are so many there and because of the narrow channel separating the humans from the seals. You can get rela-

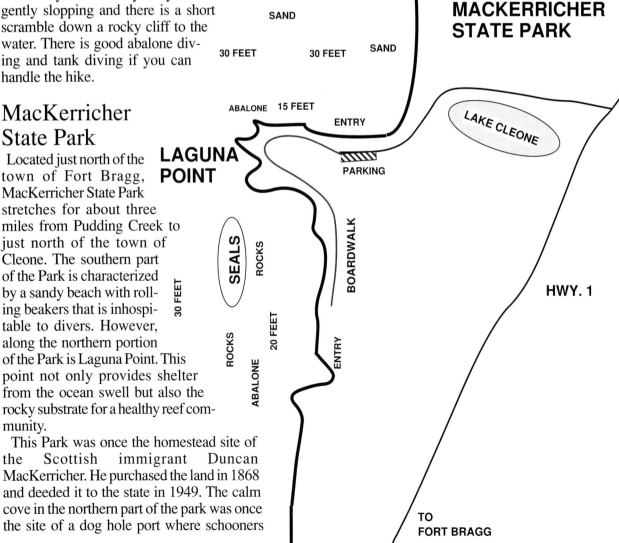

tively close to the seals, and yet they do not feel threatened because of the watery moat that separates them from you.

Most divers park in the lot on the north side of Laguna Point and walk the short distance to a wide sandy beach. After entering the water, divers should head to the left along the point. The entire north side of the point forms a rock wall that begins from the waterline and drops down to about 15 feet. The bottom then gradually drops away to between 40 and 45 feet. The deeper water has a relatively flat rock bottom with little interest for divers. There are few abalone and fish, but not a lot of critters to interest the underwater photographer. With the bottom being flat, there are few places for abalone and other animals to find shelter, so game hunters tend to clean these deeper waters out.

This contrasts the rocky walls in shallow water. The vertical walls are eroded out with an assortment of cracks, undercuts and small caves. These make perfect hiding places for a large number of abalone and other invertebrates. Seven-to eight-inch abalone are easily found in five to fifteen feet of water. The combination of calm and shallow water make this a perfect place to indoctrinate the novice hunter. The abalone, however, are not just laying on the bottom waiting for someone to scoop them up. You have to look a little harder than that.

The first place to look is back in the ledges of the rock wall. Abalone are often upside down at the entrance of the crack. These are almost never seen by swimming over the top of the reef as they are in the shadow of the ledge. Divers should swim to the base of the wall and look up. The telltale black tentacles of the abalone then often stand out against the red coralline algae above. The shallow conditions are such a good habitat for abalone that shore-pickers can still find legal-sized abalone here.

The nooks-and-crannies are also home to an assortment of non-edible, but, nonetheless, interesting critters. The shallows are covered with red coralline algae, among which numerous creatures find shelter. Small crabs and shrimp hide in the little ledges of the wall and peer out as divers pass by. Hermit crabs scurry over the algae, sometimes seeming to labor under the extra weight of their heavy shells. The better diving here is all less than 20 feet deep so there no reason to bring a tank. This place was made for free-divers and snorkelers.

An assortment of colorful nudibranchs are often seen crawling out in plain view. Their eye-catching coloration is nature's way of saying, "Take a good look at me; I don't taste very good." Aeolid nudibranchs such as the Hermissenda or the purple Spanish shawl feed on corals or other Cnidaria. The Cnidaria produce stinging cells that protect them from predators, and are of use in immobilizing prey. These nudibranchs are capable of consuming the Cnidaria, depositing the stinging cells in their gills, and using the stinging cells for their own defense.

As one swims towards the tip of Laguna Point the rock wall disappears and the shoreline breaks up into a series of massive wash rocks. These rocks make an interesting maze to swim through and their sides are covered with an assortment of algae and invertebrates. One of the more common invertebrates in the area is the giant green anemone (Anthopleura xanthogrammica). These anemones are among the largest in California waters and can grow to be some 18 inches across. In shallow water these can be quite colorful when exposed to direct sunlight. The green color is not the color of the anemone itself, but is the color of a symbiotic algae that grows within the anemone's tissues. The algae derives some security from living in the anemone and the anemone derives some nutrition from excretions of the algae.

There are a number of caves near the tip of Laguna Point that are lined with some very large green anemones. I use the word "green" here to describe the common name of this creature and not its color. These anemones are out of direct sunlight and are snow white! In the absence of sunlight the symbiotic algae does not grow and the true color of the anemone is revealed. Those of you who are expecting green anemones to really be green will find a small surprise in these caves.

The lack of access to deep water means that the fish life is sparse and generally small. This is a much better place to fish watch than to hunt. Look for small sculpins among the crevices of the reef or brightly colored greenlings among the fronds of algae.

Around the point to the south is a pretty area to dive. The bottom is made up of large rocks and boulders and offers both a firm substrate and shelter for invertebrates and fish. Abalone hunting and fishing here are quite good, and this is a nice place to critter watch as well.

MacKerricher is an interesting spot for the non-diver or for the diver seeking an after-dive hike. The beaches and dunes along the southern portion of the park are a great spot for picnicking or beachcombing. This is a relatively under-utilized park and is a great place to leave the crowds behind. At Laguna Point there is a boardwalk that extends along the more interesting parts of the park. This boardwalk protects the fragile plant life of the area, while allowing wheelchair access.

Divers pass Lake Cleone on their way to the parking lot at Laguna Point. This lake is well-stocked and is a good place to fish for rainbow trout, should ocean be too rough to dive. The lake was once a saltwater lagoon, but was cut off from the ocean when the road was built.

Within the park is located Inglenook Fen, a wetland area that is home to several endangered plants and rare and endemic insects. This is an unusual area since most wetlands are very acidic, but the underlying rocks make this a more neutral and less hostile wetland. Wild orchids, hummingbirds, egrets, great blue herons, and five species of owl are found here. This wetland is a bird watcher's heaven.

Access, Entry, and Hazards: MacKerricher State Park is located just north of the town of Fort Bragg. Turn west from Highway 1 at MEN 64.96, pay a fee at the park entrance and follow the signs to Laguna Point. One entry is a short walk from parking lot to sand beach, or one-eighth mile walk to steep rock entry that is located just south of Laguna Point. Take the boardwalk or follow the trail across the meadow. Watch for waves and surge.

Glass Beach

Fort Bragg was once a busy commercial center and remains the largest city on the Mendocino Coast. Lumbering and shipping activities began around 1885 and continue to the present day. In the late 1850s the Pomo and Coastal Yuki began to harass settlers and mills. So the federal government set up a fort here and the army rounded up the local Indians to live in it. The reservation was oversized and Indians were shipped in from other parts of California. The term "fort" is a miss-speak since there was never a stockade. Interestingly, when the land became coveted by white settlers, the Indians were moved inland to Covelo.

Much of the coastline around Fort Bragg is inaccessible due to the fencing around the Georgia Pacific Lumber Company and private housing. The only public housing is through the old town dump at Glass Beach. The name of the beach derives from the wave-polished bits of glass that are found in the surf line. For many years this site accumulated all of the trash from the thriving lumber and fishing community. As the coastline slowly succumbs to wave action, the dump area becomes exposed and glass fragments become polished by the action of surf and surge. Locals collect the bits of glass for their works of art.

Metridium anemones.

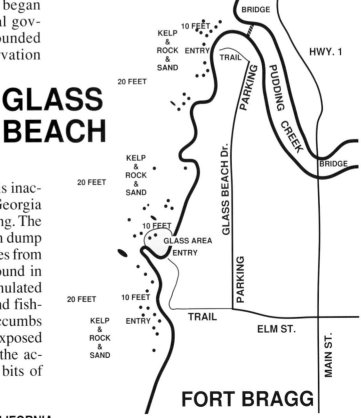

Offshore the bottom consists of rock and sand. Many of the inshore rocks are covered with eel grass. A bit farther offshore the bull kelp can be fairly thick and the rocks are covered with an assortment of sponges and coralline algae. There are plenty of abalone to be found, some to nine inches and bigger. The near-shore gravel bottom is beautiful on a sunny day as the fragments of glass reflect light in a kaleidoscope of colors.

Offshore may be found some great tank diving. Massive ridges and pinnacles spring up from the 100-foot bottom to within 50 feet of the surface. Metridium and Telia anemones dot the vertical walls and game fish abound.

Access, Entry, and Hazards: Turn west on Elm Street, the most northerly stop light on Highway 1 in the town of Fort Bragg. Proceed to Glass Beach Drive, and park on the street either at the intersection of Elm Street and Glass Beach Drive or at the end of Glass Beach Drive. Entry points are reached via a one-quarter mile, easy trail to the gravel beach. Offshore rocks provide protection from swell, but divers should be wary of big waves and swell anyway. There are no facilities. Camping may be found at Wildwood Campground, call 707-964-8297.

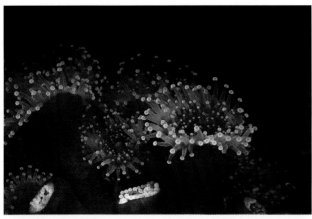
Corynactis anemones.

A diver with a Tealia anemone.

Noyo Cove

Just south of Fort Bragg is Noyo Cove and Harbor. When the parking lots of the more popular spots are full, you might find a car or two at Noyo. And I say might because you'll often find none at all. Because of this lack of diving pressure the abalone here grow big and fat. Noyo has a reputation for yielding nine-inch plus abs in relatively shallow water.

Noyo takes its name from the Pomo Indian word *No-yo-bida*, the name of their village at the mouth of the Noyo River. The first white settlers to the region peacefully coexisted with the Pomo tribes who lived south of present day Mendocino, but the Coastal Yuki to the north resisted the onslaught of settlers. The Indians continually harassed the operators of a mill at Noyo from its inception. When the mill burnt in the early 1850s the mill owners gave up and left. In 1857 complaints brought in the army and the Indians were rounded up and a reservation created for them a bit north at Fort Bragg.

In 1858 A.W. Macpherson (the same man who operated the mill at Albion) built a lumber mill and port. After several failed attempts to build a wharf that would last, ships had to be loaded the hard way, by barges that were poled out to waiting ships. Later, a tugboat was used to bring in shallow-drafted schooners that were loaded at mill side. Eventually high-strength wire became available and ships were loaded under the wire. Noyo Cove has the distinction of being the only port in California that had two wires, capable of loading both holds of a ship simultaneously. The mill was abandoned in 1880 after Macpherson died.

Noyo later developed into a busy fishing port shortly before the First World War and a small town developed. A drawbridge was built across the Noyo River. It had to be a drawbridge because the river is navigable for three miles from its mouth.

Today, Noyo is the busiest harbor in Mendocino County. The harbor offers refuge to a large fleet of fishing boats searching for albacore, salmon, sea urchins, rockfish, and dungeness crab.

Most divers park in the lot under the bridge that spans the Noyo river and walk 50 yards to the beach. The north side of the cove is well protected from the predominant northwest swell, so surf is almost non-existent at the entry. The south side of the cove is generally rougher and is nearer the main shipping channel to the harbor.

It's a long 300-yard swim from the beach to good abalone hunting grounds along the north wall of the cove. Abalone are plentiful in 10 to 25 feet of water. It's easy to pull a limit of four between eight and one-half and nine and one-half inches across. The bottom here is covered with a fine layer of silt and algae and tends not to be as interesting as other spots on the North Coast and the vis is a bit lower. Ah, but the abalone. . .

The abalone become more plentiful the closer you get to the mouth of the cove, but the big ones seem to be everywhere. Those with a fair amount of endurance and experience may choose to swim the one-half mile or so outside of the cove and to the north. Divers should concentrate on looking for abalone that are hanging upside down in small ledges or under large boulders.

Small boats may be easily launched from the beach and larger ones from the launching ramp. Divers then have the opportunity to explore some wild and untamed sites. Both north and south of the cove are uncountable little coves and points that receive few visitors. Abalone are numerous and big. Generally, there are in plain view and require very little effort to bag your limit.

Game hunting is also excellent in these remote areas. Huge lingcod, enormous cabezon and thick schools of rockfish are common. Dungeness crabs are also found in sand channels between rocky outcroppings, and rock scallops are found under ledges, away from sunlight.

Numerous offshore pinnacles can be found with the aid of a depth finder, or may be marked by kelp in the spring and summer months. These are covered with fluffy white Metridium anemones, and are home to lingcod and the occasional wolf eel.

South of the Cove are a few gorgeous homes for rent with glass on two sides, magnificent views of the ocean, and hot tubs. On calm days you can dive from your back porch, or you may drive past the trailer park to the bluffs and take one of the many trails to the water. Divers have many choices of where to enter the water and they are all good.

The bottom here is covered with pinnacles, boulders, and sculpted with deep canyons and valleys. The visibility is generally good for the area (20 to 30 feet) and the rocks are alive with color. Large

green and red anemones dot the surge channels and carpets of corynactis anemones cover the shallow portions of the pinnacles. Pink coralline algae covers the rocks in other areas, under a canopy of bull and palm kelp. On a sunny day these areas are a true joy to behold.

Commercial fishermen tend to drop their fish scraps in this area, and consequently, this is good spot for spearfishing. Larger than average lingcod and rockfish grow fat on the scraps, and are often found milling around in the open.

After the dive you can enjoy a fine seafood diner at one of the local restaurants (presuming of course that you left your speargun at home) or browse through one of the museums or shops in nearby historic Fort Bragg. My favorite way to end the day is to crawl into a hot tub and enjoy a libation, and a little abalone sushi. The sound of the surf lapping the rocks and the intensity of the sunset colors is enough to make the entire trip worthwhile even if you don't dive.

Access, Entry and Hazards: Noyo Cove is located just south of the Town of Fort Bragg. Head east on North Harbor Drive, the road just north of the bridge that crosses Highway 1 at the Noyo River. The road winds down to river level, under the bridge, and to a gravel beach. Visiting divers will find restrooms, several fine seafood restaurants that feature the local catch, and a broad gravel beach. Alternatively, you can get to a public boat launch and the Coast Guard Station by heading east on Highway 20 and taking south Harbor Drive to the river. Camping is available at nearby Pomo Campground, call 707-964-3373; and Woodside RV Park, call 707-964-3684.

Public access also be found by turning west on Del Mar Drive at MEN 60.00, the first stop light north of the intersection of Highways 1 and 20. This is called Todd Point and there are numerous access points by following trails down the bluff face. Watch for boat traffic within the cove and surgy conditions outside.

Hare Creek

Hare Creek has a pretty sandy beach that is protected from wind. The center of the cove is mostly sand with better diving to be found on the north and south points of the cove. Here, in 15 to 30 feet of water, massive rocks and boulders jut straight out of the sand bottom. Big abalone are hard to find, but eight to eight and one-half inchers are commonplace. This is a pretty area with encrusting invertebrates and small fish.

Access, Entry, and Hazards: Turn west on the Old Coast Highway (County Road 436B) from Highway 1 at MEN 59.60 on the south side of the Hare Creek Bridge. Turn right onto Cypress Road and park on the north side of the road near the end of the long, aged, redwood fence. There is public beach access between two, fenced properties. A staircase drops to the sandy beach. Watch for big waves and swell.

You may also access the area south of Hare Creek by visiting the Mendocino Coast Botanical Gardens (707-964-4352) at MEN 59.00. You'll need to pay a day use fee. Follow the well-marked and maintained trail to the rocky entry.

Yet another access is at Pine Beach Inn. Park at the turnout at MEN 57.50. It's a one-half mile hike to the rocky entry. Easier access is available if you're staying at the Pine Beach Inn, tel. 707-964-5603.

Jug Handle State Reserve

Jug Handle is a wonderful place to visit. Above the beach is a series of raised sea floors and each has its own unique habitat. One terrace contains nutrient-poor soil and is home to a Pygmy forest and carnivorous plants.

There is also excellent diving. The cove is mostly sand, so you'll need to swim past the mouth to points north and south of the cove. Here the bottom is mostly rock with huge boulders. Look for abalone in 15 to 30 feet around the rocks. They are plentiful and nine-inchers are common, although most are smaller.

Offshore, the rocky bottom is a good place to do a tank dive. Past the near-shore rocks the bottom gradually drops to 60 feet and then drops rapidly thereafter. Here you'll find vertical walls, massive rocks and pinnacles with caves and swim-throughs. The walls have a colorful assortment of invertebrate life, making this a great place for photographers. Look for rock scallops and large game fish as well. Tank diving is best done by boat from Noyo or Albion as it's a long swim to good deep water from the beach.

Access, Entry, and Hazards: Enter the Reserve from Highway 1 at MEN 56.00. Park in the large parking lot and take the trail on the north side of the parking lot. The short trail proceeds to the beach via a well-maintained staircase. You may also follow a trail to the south point of the

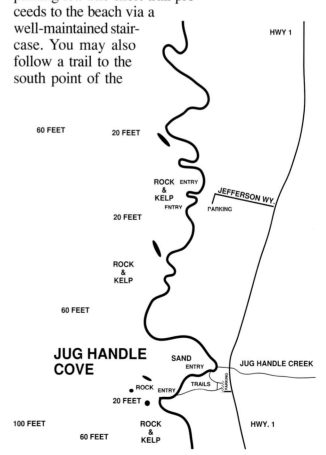

cove and climb down the cliff. This climb is particularly steep and not worth the effort since the beach access is so good. Watch for big waves and surge.

Another access point to the Reserve is near MEN 57.48. Turn west onto Jefferson Way and park where the road ends. There are several trails across the grass-covered bluff and to the water. Some trails offer easy access to the beach; others require a rope and a bit of climbing. The easiest access is along the trail beginning at the north end of the parking area.

Diver with lingcod.

Caspar Cove

Throughout most of its journey, Highway 1 hugs each and every curve of the rugged Mendocino Coast. This awesome stretch of highway treats us to some spectacular views and provides convenient access to gateways to the ocean world. Every now and then the highway disappoints us and heads inland for a short stint only to re-emerge several miles down the coast. Most of these lost stretches are privately owned and discourage exploration.

Hermit crab.

Others, however, are out-of-sight and out-of-mind, often overlooked by divers. One of these overlooked spots is Caspar Cove. This cove is long and opens to the westnorthwest. The south side of the cove can be a little rough when the northwest swell is running, but the north side is almost always calm. This is one of the best harbors in Mendocino County. The beach is very well protected and entries and exits are quite easy.

During the early 1860s a couple of store-keepers from Mendocino decided to get into lumbering and began to build a mill here. By 1862 the mill was shipping to J.G. Jackson's lumber yard San Francisco. Ships were first loaded by floating lumber out over the bar. This slow method was replaced by a chute in 1863, just in time for the 1863 depression. Jackson took over the mill in 1864.

Jackson turned the mill into a thriving business and built a 20-mile long steam railroad to Jug Handle Creek. The railroad included an 800-foot tunnel and a 150-foot high timber trestle. The Caspar Lumber Company shipped out lumber by sea for 75 years.

The floor of the cove consists of sand and gravel intermixed with rocks and boulders. It's a calm place to dive, with a few colorful anemones and other invertebrates to look at. Because of its closeness to the beach

CASPAR COVE

ABALONE
20 FEET

40 FEET
SAND
ENTRY
ENTRY
ABALONE
20 FEET
TRAIL
PARKING
CASPAR CREEK

RESERVE BOUNDARY
FROLIC WRECK

POINT CABRILLO LIGHTHOUSE

HWY. 1

RESERVE BOUNDARY

Colored dendronotid nudibranch.

The *Frolic*

The *Frolic* was a Baltimore clipper that was built to build a fortune in the lucrative drug trade with China; she was an opium-runner. Later she was put into transpacific trade.

In the spring of 1850 the *Frolic* headed east from Hong Kong with a crew of 25 and Captain Edward Horatio Faucon at the helm. In those days sailing ships rode the northern trades to the Mendocino Coast and then took advantage of the northwesterly winds to head south to San Francisco or Mexico. The *Frolic's* hold was full of Chinese silks, china, highly decorated camphor trunks, candied fruits, brass, and silver.

At about 9:30 p.m. on July 15, 1850 the *Frolic's* lookout spied the nearby Mendocino coastline. A little too nearby as it turned out. Just as the lookout called out, it was too late to turn and avoid being one of the Mendocino's first wrecks.

The rocks removed the rudder and tore a big hole in the hull. Six men refused to come down from the rigging and the rest boarded two boats and rowed south to Big River. One of the boats leaked badly, so Captain Faucon and seven crew rowed south in one boat, and the rest chose to walk. The eight men in the row boat made it safely to San Francisco and those who walked were never heard from again.

Along the San Francisco waterfront, the unlucky sailors spoke of the great treasure that went down with the ship. Harry Meiggs listened to their tales carefully and sent an expedition to salvage the *Frolic*. Would-be treasure hunters found local Indians wearing Chinese silks but never recovered any for themselves. They did, however, bring back stories of huge forests with enormous redwood trees. Thus began California's timber rush.

Today the remains of the *Frolic* reside in shallow water in a little cove just north of Caspar Lighthouse. This site was first visited by sport divers, and later by archaeologists. Dr. Thomas Layton from San Jose State University became interested in the *Frolic* when he and his students found Chinese pottery chards among Pomo Indian digs. Later, sport divers showed him where the *Frolic* could found. Much of the *Frolic's* cargo resides at the Mendocino County Museum, although it sometimes tours other maritime museums. This is one of California's most historic shipwrecks. Layton's book, *The Voyage of the* Frolic-*New England Merchants and the Opium Trade* (Stanford Press, 1997) describes the history of the ship and the wreck.

there is little game within the cove itself.

The north wall of the cove is a wonderful place to explore. There is a maze of tunnels that lead back into a private little beach. Huge rocks jut up from the 15-foot bottom to the surface and are covered with colorful marine life—giant green anemones, red coralline algae, purple kelp and many sea stars. There are a few short abalone in the cracks, but a fair number of small rockfish can be found in the shallow water. Because of the shallow water and interesting rock formations, this is a great place to free-dive or kayak.

The south side of the cove tends to get most of the wave action and is less frequently dived than the north side. On days when the swell is small this is a great place to explore and hunt. There are more and larger abalone here than on the north side, as well as more and larger fish.

The really spectacular diving is not in Caspar Cove itself but in the rugged coast just north and south of the cove. The area between the south lip of the cove and the Point Cabrillo Reserve offers some of the most spectacular game hunting in all of California. On a calm day you can snorkel on the surface and count the 9-inch abalone 15 to 20 feet below. Abalone here are so thick that you can often find one abalone clinging to the shell of another. This is a particularly pretty place to free-dive since the abalone are intermixed with giant green anemones and an assortment of colorful sea stars. Huge beds of mussels cap the offshore wash rocks.

This is also a great place for spearfishing. Huge lingcod abound in the shallow waters, particularly in the late fall and winter. Spearfishers who spurn the use of tanks will be in heaven here because of the abundance of large fish in 15 to 25 feet of water. In a little deeper water look for larger-than-average schools of blue rockfish, trophy-sized black rockfish and a few nice cabezon thrown in for fun.

If you want to hunt make sure that you stay out of the Point Cabrillo Reserve, which begins about 2500 feet north of the Point Cabrillo Lighthouse. However, if underwater photography is your game, then by all means check out the reserve. Here you will find some of the best photography in Northern California. Huge fields of fluffy white Metridium anemones, friendly game fish, and an assortment of nudibranchs will keep your strobes blazing for a great many dives.

Those with access to a boat or kayak will want to explore the offshore pinnacles outside of the cove. Here massive rock formations jut up 60 to 80 feet from a 100-to 160-foot bottom. These are covered with an assortment of colorful invertebrate life to please the most discriminating photographers and have a cornucopia of game for the taking. These offshore pinnacles are particularly interesting to game hunters because they still have a good population of rock scallops.

The topside scenery is as impressive as that below the water. The coastline is pitted with caves and arches, and harbor seals haul out on the offshore rocks. The Point Cabrillo Lighthouse is still operated by the Coast Guard, but is closed to the public. The area around the lighthouse and the Caspar State Beach is interesting to explore because of the unique rock formations and the abundance of marsh and sea birds.

Access, Entry, and Hazards: Caspar Cove is located off Point Cabrillo Drive. Exit from Highway 1 at MEN 54.71. There is limited but free parking on the edge of the beach. Small inflatable boats and kayaks may be launched. Restrooms, and a store may be found across the road at the Caspar Beach RV Campground, tel. 707-964-3306.

Access is also available by continuing on Point Cabrillo Drive to the southerly point of the cove. A steep trail leads to a little beach and several rocky shore entries. There is another public access point a bit farther down Point Cabrillo Drive. Turn west onto Otter Point Circle. There is limited parking and a public right-of-way to the bluff and a rocky entry. Great abalone hunting is just off the rocks. Watch for surge, large waves, and boat traffic.

Public access may also be found on the north side of the cove. Turn west on Caspar Street at MEN 55.50. At the "T," turn left on Caspar Road and park along the road before it turns left. Follow the well marked trail through the gate and to the beach. A sign asks you to inform the owner that you are diving here. This is a state-owned right-of-way so you need not comply, but it's a good idea to cooperate anyway.

You can gain access to the reserve by turning south onto Vega drive from Point Cabrillo Drive. Park at the end of the road and follow the trail to a small cove. There are numerous coastal deer along the trail. The reserve boundary begins at the north end of the cove. See the regulations section for reserve boundaries and rules.

Russian Gulch State Park

In 1809 Russian territory extended south to Bodega Bay, but they withdrew in 1841 when the sea otter became virtually extinct and other marine mammals were no longer worth hunting. The Russians left little to remember them by, just the remains of a fort (Fort Ross in Sonoma County) and several names on the map. One of the Russian strongholds is now called Russian Gulch and was located just north of the town of Mendocino. Russian Gulch has a long history of shipping and logging. The remains of a wharf may be found along the north side of the cove. The port once had two slide chutes and a wire. At least two schooners were sunk here.

This pleasant little cove is a California state park, and should not be confused with the Russian Gulch in Sonoma County. The latter is where Highway 1 makes that famous hairpin turn about five miles north of Jenner.

This state park offers two distinctly different diving experiences. Divers may follow the road that passes beneath the bridge that traverses Russian Gulch, and to a sandy beach. The Cove here is "W"-shaped, and the gulch empties to the northern wing of the "W." The main cove is mostly gravel and silt with a few boulders. Depths range from 15 to 40 feet. Attached to the boulders are a few wisps of bull kelp and a few abalone. There are also a few fish here.

Better diving may be found along the north point of the cove. This area is quite sheltered from the northwest wind and swell and is a very pleasant place to dive. Here one finds a rocky bottom with canyons and valleys. There is a fair population of abalone 10 to 30 feet deep. There are no real monsters to be had, but a limit of seven and a-half to eight-inchers may be plucked with a minimum of effort.

On calm days the best diving is along the southern point of the cove and in the adjoining cove to the south. This area is open to the northwest swell and can get ugly on rough days. However, on calm days you will find few dives that are more enjoyable. Here the bottom is rugged with deep canyons and vertical mini-walls. The walls create a maze-like structure that is a joy to explore. Throughout the rocky maze are thousands of abalone. Abalone here are both larger and more numerous than in nearby areas, all in only 20 to 30 feet of water.

Photographers will also enjoy this area. Orange sea cucumbers give color to the rocky walls and surge channels, along with large anemones and encrusting sponges. Those with a little patience will find an assortment of little nudibranchs and tame fish.

Another diving area at Russian Gulch is off the point on the northern side of the park. Offshore, free-divers will find a healthy population of large abalone and fish. Due to the hike involved, few expend the energy to haul tanks out this far. A blow hole is located on the bluffs near the entry.

Access, Entry, and Hazards: The state park is located off Highway 1 at MEN 53.00. Divers take the third right past the park kiosk to reach a well-protected sand beach with restrooms. Small inflatable boats and kayaks are easily launched here. More rugged rocky-beach entries may be found by taking the second right past the entry kiosk. Park on the bluff and hike down the many trails to rocky beach entries. Call 800-444-PARK for camping reservations. There are restrooms and outdoor showers near the beach entry.

500D

This spot is also called Jack Peters Cove and is part of Russian Gulch State Park. This is one of the beach dives in Mendocino County where you will want to take your tanks. A short trail leads to a rocky entry, and deep water may be found a short swim from shore.

Vertical walls drop from the shoreline to 40 feet. Pinnacles dot the bottom 40 to 100 feet offshore, some break the surface, others come up to 5 to 10 feet. The tops of the pinnacles are covered with coralline algae, and abalone are common on the tops of the pinnacles and within cracks on the walls. This area gets a lot of abalone divers so you will have to hunt a bit

to find big abalone, but eight-inchers are common.

The rocky bottom and vertical walls are very pretty with large anemones and colorful sponges. There are large lingcod, cabezon, greenlings and giant Pacific octopus. Directly off the entry is an underwater arch big enough to drive a truck through. A short swim will put divers in 60 to 80 feet of water.

Access Entry, and Hazards: To reach the 500D entry turn west from Highway 1 at MEN 52.00 on to County Road 500D. Drive to the end of the road, make a U-turn and park along the turnout 200 yards from the end of the road. Parking is limited to three or four cars. There is a short, moderately steep to very steep hike to rocky entries, and there are no facilities. The easiest entry (and the one you want to use if you intend on tank diving) may be found by heading north from the turnout in the middle of the road, and following the trail to the right. Proceed down the gently-sloping rock surface and enter to the right. There are other trails that are much steeper. Bring a rope if you want to try these out. The trail that begins at the end of 500D puts you into the southern part of Russian Gulch Cove

Another entry is at the north side of Jack Peters Gulch at MEN 51.54. Park along the road on the west side of Highway 1 just south of the bridge that crossed Jack Peters Gulch, or on Lansing Street. Follow the very steep trail on the north side of the bridge to a rocky entry.

A diver glides through thick kelp.

Mendocino Headlands State Park

During the late 1800s the biggest city on the Redwood Coast was the town of Mendocino. At first the area was called Big River after the large stream just south of the present-day city. In 1851 a gentleman by the name of Harry Meiggs became interested in opening a mill along the coast after Captain Richardson began his adventure at Albion. Meiggs was originally a Brooklyn lumber dealer and made a bit of money early on shipping lumber to San Francisco, and he was the original subdivider of San Francisco's North Beach. He found a good watershed with tremendous stands of redwood along Big River and established a mill there by 1852. The town of Meiggsville grew up around the mill.

The first mill was located at the point where the town of Mendocino now sits. The location proved to be as reliable a port that one could find in that part of the coast but did not prove to be a good spot for a mill. Another mill was constructed in the river flats, just east of the present-day bridge. By the time he had the second mill completed, the gold rush had petered out, the price and demand for lumber was down, and California was into its first depression. So in 1854 Meiggs grabbed what cash he could and headed for Tahiti.

Two of Meiggs' creditors, Ford and Williams, ended

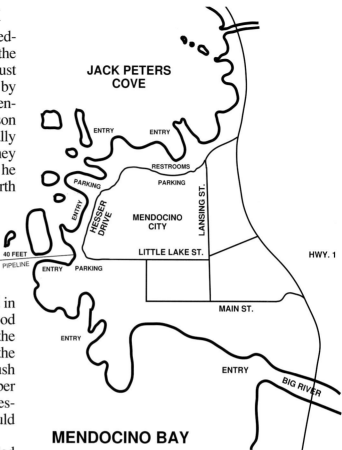

Hilton's nudibranch.

up with the property, turned it into a thriving business, and renamed the town Mendocino. Williams retired in 1912 and sold out to the Union Lumber Company, who operated a mill there until the 1930s. For nearly 80 years Mendocino was an active port. It was routine to have two or three schooners loading or waiting to load, and at times six or seven could be in port. The landing was located beneath the bluff on which the town currently sits.

Today few divers frequent Mendocino Headlands. I'm not sure if all of the pricey shops and tourists scare them away or if they don't like climbing down bluffs. Either way, when the beaches of Van Damme or Russian Gulch are packed to the gills, there may only be a few divers at the headlands.

There are numerous entries from the headlands and all of them can get you to good diving. One of my favorites is called the Pipeline, named after an iron pipe that runs out to sea from a cubical, concrete structure on the beach. The pipeline runs out a couple hundred yards and makes navigation a cinch.

Jump off the rocks into 10 to 15 feet of water. On one side of the point is a real pretty arch, some 20 feet high, and on the other is a 30-foot wide surge channel. Depths in the channel run 10 to 15 feet, and there are plenty of abalone beneath the entry point. A little bit from shore the bottom drops to 40 feet. This area and the offshore rocks are very pretty. Giant green anemones and red Telia anemones dot the rocky walls. This area is swept by currents and the water movement gives this spot a bit better diversity and concentration of marine life than nearby sites. Abalone here are numerous, but small (seven to eight inches) and a bit deeper (25-40 feet) than inshore spots.

As you follow the pipeline further, it descends over some very pretty rocky walls where it ends at a 60-foot sand bottom. This is a fair to good place to spearfish for rockfish.

Other entries off the Headlands are not nearly so dramatic but worth doing. The abalone at these other sites are not so numerous, or large but are shallow enough for beginners. The other entries are a bit more protected as well.

Access, Entry, and Hazards: There are several entries located off Hessler Drive in Mendocino. One is located directly behind the restrooms on the north side of town, two at the far westerly bends in the road and another at the end of Main Street. The parking area at the most southerly bend in Hessler Drive is the Pipeline (See map for details). All entries involve a short to moderate hike and an intermediate climb down to the water and a rocky entry. Watch for big waves, swell, and strong currents, particularly on the more westerly entries. When the surf is up there is a

Jack Peters Cove.

very fast current that runs offshore at the pipeline entry. This area can be very dangerous since it is exposed the northwesterlies, and the wave energy can be concentrated by surge channels.

Another entry is via Big River Beach parking lot. There is a long but level hike across the beach to the entry and a long swim to good diving near the headlands. This is a good spot to launch a kayak or small inflatable boat.

Van Damme State Park

Located just south of the town of Mendocino, Van Damme State Park has a well protected cove with a wide gravel beach that is now surrounded by second-growth redwoods. This is certainly one of the nicest public beach and camping areas on the north coast and has some great diving to boot. It's hard to imagine that this peaceful little beach was once a bustling commercial center.

The cove at Van Damme State Park was originally called Little River and was initially overlooked as a site of a lumber mill because of the small stands of nearby redwood. It was first developed as a port to ship fresh elk meat back to San Francisco. As the elk herds dwindled, the area became a cattle ranch and later a potato farm. By 1864 the timber around better sites such as Albion and Big River began to thin out and a lumber mill was established. The landing always went by the name Little River.

The mill remained in business for over 20 years, right alongside a shipyard that turned out 19 schooners. This was one of the few sites on the North Coast where it was practical to build a wharf for the purpose of loading and unloading ships, as wharves rarely lasted a single season at most other sites. The wharf at Little River lasted over 20 years, a testament to the degree of protection that the cove offers. Chutes and high wires were also utilized on the north and south points of the cove.

During the 1850s a mill worker's son named Charles Van Damme went off looking for fame and fortune and found it as the owner of the Richmond-San Rafael ferry line. Charles loved the area where he grew up and later in life bought up all of the land surrounding the cove. He willed the land to the state upon his death and required that the beach and cove would remain free for all to enjoy. Ironically, right after the creation of the state park the native Indians were run off the land. No camping is allowed on the beach.

Today, little remains of the area's colorful past. In the center of the cove, inshore and north of Key Hole rock, may be found piles of ballast rocks. These were used to weigh down schooners that left empty from San Francisco and were dropped in the cove as the ships filled with lumber. These are now covered with abalone in 30 to 35 feet of water. Other signs of commercial activity has been removed, except for a little wreckage from the wooden hulled steam schooner, *Sunol*, in the southern part of the cove.

It is not, however, tales of schooners and sailing that attracts folks here, it is the excellent diving. The pair of large wash rocks named Key Hole and Top Hat and the surrounding smaller rocks create an extensive reef system that effectively protect the cove from all but the worst of winter storms. When every other spot on the north coast is "blown out," Van Damme will often be still diveable. Just offshore are a wealth of colorful invertebrates, large fish and curious marine mammals.

The southern part of the cove has rocky areas separated by patches of sand. The predominant beds of bull and giant kelp mark the rocky areas and have been pretty well picked over for game but still have an assortment of invertebrates to look at. Nudibranchs

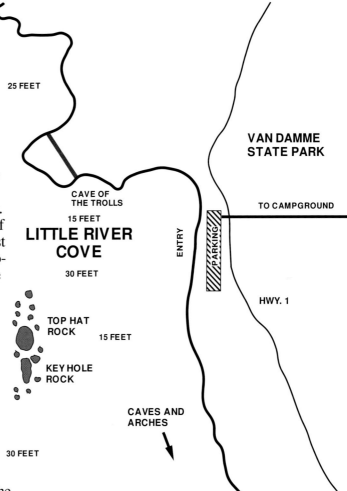

25 FEET

VAN DAMME
STATE PARK

CAVE OF
THE TROLLS

15 FEET

LITTLE RIVER
COVE

30 FEET

TO CAMPGROUND

ENTRY

PARKING

HWY. 1

TOP HAT
ROCK

15 FEET

KEY HOLE
ROCK

CAVES AND
ARCHES

30 FEET

such as the horned nudibranch, clown nudibranch, and the sea lemon may be found in great numbers in the shallow water. Rocks are covered with palm kelp and coralline algae that gently sway back and forth in the surge.

The northern part of the cove is mostly gravel with little of interest for divers until one reaches the north wall. Here is a small bed of giant kelp

Kayaking at Van Damme.

Little River Cove.

Blood star.

Sea lion.

with an assortment of rose and giant green anemones. Swim along the north face of the cove to find the entrance to a large tunnel. It is about 20 feet tall, 10 feet wide, 100 feet long and is half filled with water. The tunnel is great fun to swim through on calm days and is an eerie experience with the constant but mild surge picking you up and down and the sound of the echoing surf.

Upon exiting the tunnel, swim 100 yards to the right to the next small cove. Numerous but small lingcod and cabezon may be seen here in shallow water. This is a pretty area to explore with deep channels and caves, and a thick growth of red coralline algae cover the shallow rocks. An abundance of 7-to 8-inch abalone may be found within cracks in the rocky walls, 10 to 15 feet deep. Even larger specimens may be found in deeper water.

On calm days the best diving to be found here is on the outside of Key Hole and Top Hat Rocks. Just beyond the rocks are a series of depressions that are filled with large abalone in 20 feet of water. Giant green anemones dot the bottom and some game fish are found here. The bottom drops off rapidly to over 80 feet and the rock walls are covered with fluffy white Metridium anemones and large lingcod sulk about. Watch for sea lions as they cruise through the kelp beds. Pelagic animals such as ocean sunfish and medusa jellyfish are also often spotted here.

Don't forget to take a little time to explore the topside part of the park as well. There is a trail leading a Pygmy forest, where the poor soil conditions have lead to an area where the trees are severely stunted. There is also a peat bog with an assortment of carnivorous plants, including the rare sundew.

Access, Entry, and Hazards: Located at MEN 48.03, and there is ample, free parking right off Highway 1. Outdoor showers and restrooms are available on the beach and there is campground in the park. Call 800-444-PARK for reservations. Watch for surge and boat traffic. The kelp bed may be thick in summer.

You may also get to the cove by turning west into the dirt lot at MEN 48.25 at Rachel's Inn. Park in the lot and follow the paved road for 100 yards and then a trail to the left. The trail ends at north end of Little River Beach.

Another access point to the area north of Van Damme State Park is opposite Gordon Lane at MEN 49.00. Park along the fence and hike two-thirds of a mile through a forest and grassy bluff to the cliff. There are several ways to the water. Be careful; they involve some climbing.

Buckhorn Cove

Some of the most rugged and beautiful coastline in all of California lies between Van Damme and Albion. Divers with boats should take the time to explore this area. However, the best way to experience this coastline is by kayak. Kayaks may be launched from either Van Damme, Albion or the public access trail at Buckhorn Cove.

Surrounding Buckhorn Cove are a group of many large rocks or small islands. The many rocks create a labyrinth of protected coves, secluded beaches, and hidden passageways. Large caves and arches are common throughout the area. Some caves go 100 feet or more into the bluffs; others provide shortcuts between coves.

The visibility is generally better in this area when compared to the nearby, larger coves, and more and bigger fish and abalone may be found here as well. The bottom topography presents a rugged terrain with deep canyons, small caves and tall pinnacles that jut up from the 50-foot bottom to near the surface. These have acquired a colorful growth of encrusting invertebrates.

Near shore the bottom is sand in between rock walls, vertical-sided mini-pinnacles, and rocky patch reefs. Abalone are numerous and large (eight to nine inches). This is a great area to pick abalone when the surf is

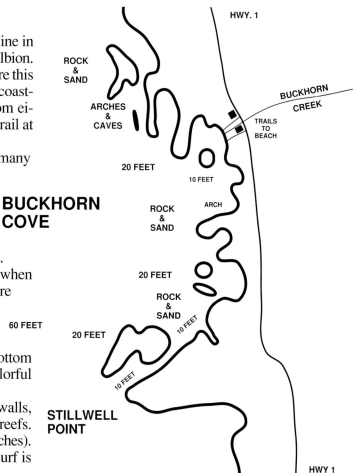

Cabezon.

up because the offshore rocks disperse the wave's energy before it reaches the beach.

Outside of the cove are a group of rather impressive pinnacles known as Colby Reef. These can be easily located by wisps of kelp that come to the surface. There is a thick bed of kelp along the coast, but tiny kelp beds offshore of the main bed often mark a pinnacle. After the winter storms rip out the kelp beds, the pinnacles can only be found with a depth finder.

Colby reef is a massive rock structure that begins in about 20 feet of water and drops to well over 100 feet. The reef is carved with deep canyons, caves, swim-throughs, and the rock walls are covered with Metridium anemones. This is another good spot to see rockfish and lings.

Access, Entry and Hazards: Park along the west side of Highway 1 at MEN 47.00. Walk along the road south for 100 feet and follow one of two trails to the beach. Should you take the most northerly trail you are trespassing, but nobody seems to care. The southerly trail is public access and runs between two fences. Please respect the privacy of the land owners. The beach is protected from big waves by offshore rocks and offers a very protected entry. The best abalone diving is reached by swimming or paddling through the cave on the south end of the beach into the next cove. This beach is a great place to launch kayaks, but not boats. There are no facilities. Watch for big waves and surge when you leave the protection of the rocks. Colby Reef is one and one-half miles north of Albion and one-half mile offshore of Stillwell Point on the south side of Buckhorn Cove(39° 14.983' N, 123° 47.797' W).

Albion Cove

Next time you visit Mendocino County, pay particular attention to the bridge over the Albion River. Passengers (not the driver, please) will get a good look at a long, thin cove. You are sure to see a few commercial fishing boats and a few inflatable dive boats puttering into or out of the cove.

Seems strange that many divers skip over this cove on their way to points north, and their only enjoyment of the cove comes from a brief glimpse as they pass over the bridge. Those who own a small boat or kayak will want to check out Albion Cove in a little more detail.

Like most protected coves along the Mendocino Coast, Albion played a major part in shaping the history of the area. Captain William Richardson took a fancy to the property, promptly forged a Mexican land grant, and took possession.

Apparently, that was quite a common thing to do at the time. During the summer of 1851, he began the construction of a mill and landing. By June of 1852 the first load of lumber from Albion reached San Francisco. Richardson quickly ran into financial problems and his property was subdivided and sold off. That created a problem for many when the forged land grant papers were discovered. The landing and mill eventually became the property of A.W. Macpherson who turned the venture into a profitable business. Macpherson, by-the-way, also operated the mill at Noyo at the same time.

By the end of the 19th century Albion was at its heyday. A pier was built for ships to tie off, and what is now a flat beach was covered with a mill, lumber piles, a hotel, general store and mill offices. Every couple of years a fire, flood or tidal wave would take out the lumber mill, dock, and buildings; and the whole settlement would have to be rebuilt. A mill operated off-and-on until about 1920 when the logging business was shut down for good.

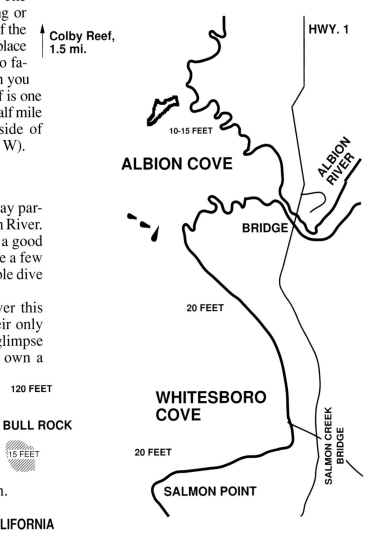

120 FEET

BULL ROCK

15 FEET

Colby Reef, 1.5 mi.

HWY. 1

10-15 FEET

ALBION COVE

ALBION RIVER

BRIDGE

20 FEET

WHITESBORO COVE

20 FEET

SALMON CREEK BRIDGE

SALMON POINT

Albion Cove.

You would never know by looking at the cove today that it was once a busy little seaport. Little is left from the once thriving community, except the remains of the old wharf along the south side of the beach and numerous anchors in the water along the south side of the cove. The anchors are there not because a ship had sunk, but rather they were deliberately placed there and were used to secure schooners as they took on cargo.

Today Albion provides access for divers and fisherpersons. The cove has a wide sandy beach, well protected from wind and swell. Divers may park in a day-use area near the cove, and carry their gear across the wide, sandy beach. The center of the cove is mostly sand and of little interest to divers. Pilings still stick out of the sand beach and mark the site of the old wharf. The south side of the cove is often rough, is in the boating channel, and should be avoided by divers.

The north side of the cove is often calm and is a fun place in which to poke around. Free divers can find abalone and a few small fish in 15 to 20 feet of water. The rocks are mostly covered with coralline algae. This can be a pretty place to snorkel, particularly on a sunny day.

The cove is about one-half mile long, a long swim to open water. To be honest, if you don't have access to a boat of kayak there are a whole lot better spots to dive in Mendocino. Those who own a small boat or kayak, or sign on a charter boat, will really enjoy this area.

Whitesboro Cove to the south is a particularly fun area for free-divers to explore. Deep channels (15 to 30 feet), and overhangs provide a home for a variety of critters. Wolf-eels, kelpfish and an assortment of crabs and nudibranchs will delight the photographer/sightseer. The shallow waters are a breeding ground for some of the healthiest abalone beds in the North Coast. From the surface you can often pick-and-choose among which 9-incher you will pull, a mere 10 to 15 feet below. Even novice divers can pull two abalone with one breath, because often there is one clinging to the shell of another.

One of the best dives near Albion is Bull Rock. This pinnacle is offshore of the south end of Whitesboro Cove. The pinnacle begins in about 15 feet from the surface and drops in steps to 120 feet. Numerous smaller pinnacles surround the main one, separated by deep valleys. The top of the pinnacles are covered with bull and palm kelp, interspersed with beds of strawberry anemones and a few large Telia anemones.

In deeper waters divers encounter fields of Metridium anemones and fields of encrusting sponges, cup corals and rock scallops. Scallops begin to appear at about 60 feet. At this depth they are small and hard to find. As one goes deeper they get bigger and more numerous. At a depth of around 100 feet it's easy to get your limit of 10 in a few minutes. These pinnacles are a great place for spearfishing. Schools of blue rockfish and larger than average lingcod are common. I've seen divers get their limit of blues here on a single tank.

Access, Entry, and Hazards: Albion Cove is located at MEN 43.93, about four miles south of Mendocino off Hwy. 1. A steep, windy road takes you to Albion flats with boat launching facilities and public (fee) access. Two RV parks are on the Albion River: Albion River Campground (707-937-0606) on the flats, and Schooner's (707-937-5707) is on the left and along the river. Beware of boat traffic while diving within the cove, and waves and surge in the outer areas. Divers should stay well away from the boat lanes. Bull Rock is off the south side of Whitesboro Cove (39° 12.931' N, 123° 47.233' W).

In addition, you may dive the area north of Albion by parking a MEN 45.24 at the Heritage House. Park near the end of the redwood wooden fence and walk south to find the trailhead. This is a public access, but please respect the privacy of the adjacent land owners. A well maintained trail and staircase leads to a cobblestone beach. You may dive the rocks in the center of the cove or both north and south of the cove. There is good abalone diving for eight to eight and a half inches and some good spearfishing for lingcod near shore. To stay at the upscale Heritage House call 707-937-5885.

Navarro River Beach

This public beach is located at the intersection of Highway 1 and Highway 128. The beach and cove offer protected entries to good diving just offshore. Navarro was an active port and lumber mill during the last part of the 19th and early 20th centuries. The dog hole was called Wendling and the mill sat on the flats on the south side of the river. This was a profitable operation until the mill closed in the 1930s.

The visibility in the shallow water just off the beach is poor due to the outfall of the Navarro River. Better visibility may be found among the rock piles 200 yards farther from shore. Abalone and some fish may be found among the rocks, but the better diving and visibility can be found on the rocky point to the north.

A large arch is located under the largest rock that is still connected to the north point of the cove. On nautical charts this is marked as the "Navarro Arch." Outside of the north point is a pretty, rocky area with vertical walls, pinnacles, and canyons that run out to sea. Look for abalone up to nine inches at the bottom of the rock walls, along with schools of rockfish. The invertebrate life is a bit thin compared to other Mendocino sites, but this is a good place for free divers to enjoy the shallow water (10 to 40 feet) and a great place for scuba diving if you have a boat or kayak. Those with kayaks or boats will enjoy exploring the four-mile stretch of coastline between Navarro and Albion.

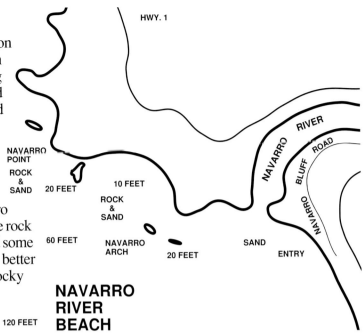

NAVARRO RIVER BEACH

Access, Entry, and Hazards: From Highway 1 at MEN 40.18 take Navarro Bluff Road west. This road begins on the south side of the bridge that crosses the Navarro River. At the end of the road is day parking and a campground, but the only facilities are pit toilets. Bring you own water. There is a fee for camping and reservations are not accepted. Either wade across the river and enter south of the point, or enter in the river and ride it out to sea and swim north. Watch for big surge and swell. This beach can get mighty rough.

A free-diver ascends with an abalone.

Elk

South of Navarro lies a rugged coastline that is certainly among the most breathtaking in the entire state. Offshore, the coastline is spotted with islands and large rocks that create a labyrinth of passageways with caves and arches. Highway 1 winds along high above the beach, and often on the edge of a vertical cliff. There is plenty of good diving here, but no trespassing signs and locked gates keep divers from the water. The only public access in the area is in the town of Elk, an area with a history as interesting as the diving is good.

By 1851 the rush for redwood was going strong and lumber mills were beginning to pop up everywhere. Since the lumbermen needed to eat and there were no supermarkets in the area, hunting camps were established between lumber mills. So Captain Richardson sent out Francisco Faria and Nathaniel Smith, and they set up camp a few miles south of Navarro. Nathaniel, as it turns out, was one of the few persons of color on the coast at the time and the spot became known as Cuffey's Cove. At that time Cuffey was common slang for a person of color. Meanwhile, the Greenwood brothers established their camp about a mile south.

Francisco had a yearn to farm the area and bought up some of Richardson's land when it was subdivided. Shortly afterwards Richardson's falsified land grant was discovered. Francisco was left holding a worthless piece of paper and had little more than squatters rights to the property. He quickly traded the land to an Irishman by the name of James Kenney for a few head of cattle. Kenney began a cattle ranch and potato farm and was said to have made a fair profit. In fact, Cuffey's Cove potatoes were reputed to be the best in the state, and fetched a high price in San Francisco markets.

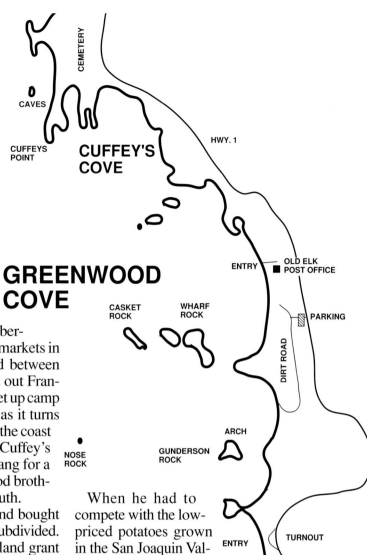

When he had to compete with the low-priced potatoes grown in the San Joaquin Valley and the land was farmed out, Kenney began to log up nearby stream beds. He eventually owned two working saw mills with a four-mile stretch of railroad to bring lumber to the mill. This port was one of the most active in the area with two chutes going all the time and a town with hotels, several stores, saloons, a restaurant and a candy store. At

On the beach at Elk.

Vermilion rockfish.

its peak Cuffey's Cove was second in size only to Mendocino.

Later, a lumberman named L.E. White took a fancy to the land just south of Cuffey's Cove. White owned the mill at Salmon Creek, had taken all the redwood he could get, and wanted to move his operation to a better site. White offered to buy Kenney's landing, but he and Kenney could never come to terms over the price. So, White put in a landing at Greenwood and built a mill, a landing with a wharf, and a rail road to bring lumber to his mill from the watershed south of Greenwood Creek. The new town began to grow and needed a post office. There was already a post office with the name "Greenwood," so Kinney took the name "Elk" after the creek a bit to the south. At first it was called the "Elk Post Office at Greenwood," but later everyone started calling the town Elk. As Elk grew, the residents of Cuffey's Cove eventually moved the mile south. All that is left of Cuffey's Cove today is a cemetery and Kenney's old residence.

Greenwood Cove today is state-owned and has good public access. However, due the outfall from Greenwood creek, the visibility in the cove is poor and the bottom sandy. However, divers will find excellent diving north and south of the main cove. The bottom around Cuffey's Cove to the north is rocky, with an abundance of invertebrate and fish life. Rocky walls begin at the water line and drop vertically to a sand bottom, 10 to 40 feet below.

This area is reputed to have more and bigger abalone than anywhere in the state. I suspect these rumors got started because the area is so hard to get to. They continue because they are true! In 15 to 20 feet of water divers can find a great many abalone between 9 and 10 inches, with occasional monsters over 10 inches. It is sometimes hard to find abalone under 9 inches. This is also an excellent area for spearfishing for lingcod, and red and blue rockfish.

Rocky bluffs under the Cuffey's Cove Cemetery are riddled with caves and tunnels. A 15-foot tall cathedral-sized chamber is located under the western edge of the cemetery. Four separate tunnels lead to this main chamber. This is a great area to explore by kayak.

South of Greenwood is a pretty area to dive. Near shore the bottom remains at 10 to 15 feet for some distance, then drops to 25 to 30 feet. The bottom is sand with huge rocks sprinkled about. This is a good place for hunting abalone, particularly deeper water.

Offshore of the south end of Greenwood Cove is Nose Rock. The water surrounding the rock is 60 feet deep and is a great place to hunt for rockfish. Big abalone, Metridium and Telia anemones are everywhere. Around the rock are plentiful abs in 15 to 20 feet of water.

Access, Entry, and Hazards: Public access is very limited in the Elk area. There is free, public parking directly across from the Elk Store on the west side of Highway 1. A trail leads to the ocean and splits. The path to the right (north) leads to a nice little picnic area with a good view of the cove. Behind the picnic tables are remnants of the old wire chutes that once were used to load schooners. The trail to the left (south) goes past an outhouse and gradually descends to the beach where another outhouse is located. This is a good spot to launch kayaks to explore sites north and south of the cove. Vehicles are not permitted on the beach, so boat launching is not possible.

The trail north from the parking lot winds behind the old Elk Post Office, over the bluff to a point, and down to the water. This descent is dangerous and locals have left a rope in place to aid divers.

The third access point is just south of town at a turnout bordered by mile markers MEN 37.17 and 37.07. There is ample parking and a very steep and dangerous trail to the beach. Locals have left a rope in place to help you on your way down.

Watch for big waves and surge here, and pay attention to conditions that can change rapidly. Except for the Greenwood Beach access, expect to climb down a steep and dangerous cliff. You may want to bring a rope in case the permanent ones have vanished.

Arena Rock

Arena Rock is one of the most spectacular sites in Mendocino County. There are actually two rocks. Arena Rock comes within 20 feet of the surface and drops vertically to about 120 feet. Little Arena Rock is a bit smaller and deeper than the Arena Rock. Its top begins about 50 feet and drops vertically as well to a flat, rocky bottom. Both rocks are flat-topped and are honeycombed with caves.

These rocks are a magnet for marine life. Huge Metridium anemones dot the rock along with corynactis, and large numbers of huge rock scallops. Trophy lingcod may be found back in the holes and in caves. Thick schools of rockfish circle the rocks, and unusual invertebrates abound. This is a world class dive spot.

Access, Entry, and Hazards: Access by boat only from Arena Cove or Albion. Watch for big waves, very strong currents and access to deep water. Divers should check their anchors and leave someone on board who knows how to operate the boat should divers get down current. Those with GPS will find Little Arena Rock at 38° 58.640' N, 123° 44.903' W. Arena Rock is about 100 yards to the magnetic southwest.

Arena Cove

Point Arena was first named Punta de las Arenas, or "Sand Point," after the large stretch for sand directly north of the point, now called Manchester Beach. In 1868 Rafael Garcia operated a mill at the mouth of Garcia River which empties into the ocean just north of Point Arena. Garcia's mill was located near the junction of Lighthouse Road and Highway 1. The mill had a wooded fume that allowed logs to be floated from inland areas to the mill. Dog Holers were loaded via chutes.

A lighthouse was built in 1871. In 1906 Point Arena moved north about three feet and the resulting earthquake severely damaged the lighthouse. So, the lantern was removed, reassembled on a temporary stage, and put into service. The old tower was then knocked down, another concrete structure built in the same place, and the lantern replaced. The entire process took about two years. The current tower has seen over 90 years of service and the lantern nearing 130 years old.

To the south of the point is Arena Cove. This cove is well-protected from the northwesterly wind and swell and makes a fine anchorage. This is a commercial port where fishing boats and fish and urchins are landed here as well.

The cove itself is shallow (less than 40 feet), and its shale and sand bottom begins at the waterline and gently slopes off to deeper water. On the south side of the cove is a thin kelp bed in about 15 feet of water. The rock bottom is flat with a covering of palm kelp in some places. Marine life here is generally uninteresting, abalone are sparse, and you will have to hunt a bit to find one. However, abs here are gregarious, so once you have found one,

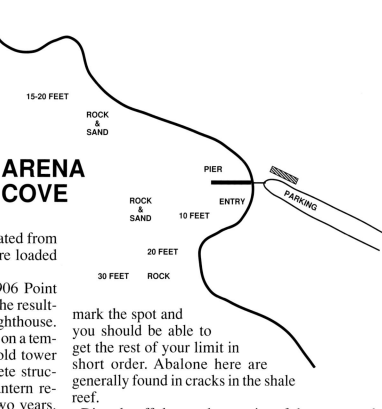

mark the spot and you should be able to get the rest of your limit in short order. Abalone here are generally found in cracks in the shale reef.

Directly off the southern point of the cove, and about 300 yards offshore, is another shale reef in 20 to 30 feet of water that drops off to 60 feet. Abalone here are larger and more common.

On the north side of the cove lie a series of rocky ridges to about 30 feet. The ridges run north to south and are home to a good assortment of lingcod, rockfish and abalone. Conditions here are calmer than are found on the south side of Arena Cove.

Commercial fishermen claim that the best abalone hunting around is on their moorings. Diving in the cove is not the best due to the poor visibility and lack of interesting things to look at. The cove, however, is an excellent spot to launch your boat to explore sites north and south of the cove, or to blow a tank when the northwesterly swell is running big.

Access, Entry, and Hazards: From Highway 1 south of the town of Point Arena, take Port Road west to Arena Cove. There you will find plenty of free parking, public restrooms with fee showers, a large beach and several restaurants. There is a particularly good pier with a boat hoist that will handle rather large craft. The pier is open April 15th to September 30th. Watch for boat traffic within the cove, and strong currents with rough and surgy conditions outside of the cove. Camping is available at the nearby Manchester Beach KOA, call 707-882-2375, or 800-562-4188.

Point Arena pier.

Anchor Bay

Anchor Bay is located north of Gualala and access to the ocean is through the private campground that is just north of town. Nestled in a large stand of redwoods and amidst one of the prettier parts of the coast, this campground has a reputation of being a friendly haven which caters to both divers and fishermen alike.

The campground empties directly onto a large beach and, due to a eastern cut in the coastline, faces directly south. This provides excellent sun exposure, even in the winter months for the sunbathers. The bay also provides protection from the prevailing northwest swell, making it one of the calmest dive sites on the coast during the summer months. However, the bay opens directly into the prevailing southern, winter storm swell.

This geography makes Anchor Bay a safe summer anchorage and was once a dog hole port. The westerly point was used to load waiting ships by means of a long chute, that was held in place with a giant crane. Anchor Bay was first called Fish Rocks Landing by the mid 1800s settlers after the two small islands just west of the bay. The origin of that name is unknown but probably reflects the good fishing here.

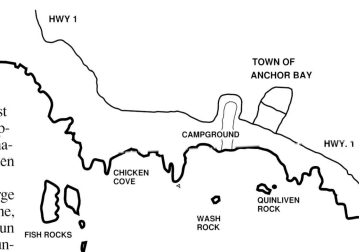

ANCHOR BAY

During the Coast Guard Survey of 1853 the bay was renamed Havens Anchorage after one of the ship's officers. His name still marks the neck just north of Fish Rocks. The name Anchor Bay was later taken from the general store located there.

Anchor Bay was not considered to be a hazardous place for ships and no lighthouse was ever constructed here. Captains knew to stay far out to sea in this area to avoid the truly treacherous Saunders Reef and Point Arena, located north of Anchor Bay. Nonetheless over

Spanish shawl nudibranchs.

a dozen ships have met their demise here. One of the larger ships lost here was the 150-foot steam ship *Crescent City,* which ran aground on Fish Rocks January 29, 1903 and the most recent was the Vietnamese fishing boat, the *Vung Tau,* which washed up on the beach November 3, 1988. None of these wrecks have remained intact, but wreckage may be found in deep water west of Fish Rock. Artifacts are still found by those persistent few who systematically search the channel between the rocks and the mainland.

Fish Rocks themselves consist of two main rocks, the outer one being 150 feet high and the inner 100 feet high with a narrow beach between. A large colony of California sea lions reside here. Old sailors used to say that all one had to do to make Fish Rock Landing in the fog was to listen for the barking of the sea lions.

It is not the wrecks that draws divers to Anchor Bay but the abundance of abalone and fish. The best diving is on the open water side of Fish Rocks where the bottom begins in 20 feet of water and slopes to over 100 feet to a sand bottom. This area is highly textured with tall pinnacles, deep cracks and high-sided canyons. The tops of the pinnacles are covered with palm kelp which wave to-and-fro in the surge and below the kelp are colonies of red Corynactis anemones. Large rose and giant green anemones dot the surge channels. Many of the pinnacles and walls, between 40 and 70 feet deep, are covered with fluffy white Metridium anemones. In some places these anemones cover large areas, appearing as a field of over-sized cotton balls extending out to the limit of visibility.

This area is the most productive for spearfishers, with large stringers of lingcod in the 10-to 15-pound range consistently being taken and an occasional 30-to 40-pound monster. Good sized cabezon and rockfish can also be found here in abundance. These fish find shelter in the many nooks and crannies of the reef or swim in and out of the kelp beds. Pole fishermen generally do well drift fishing in deep water just south of Fish Rocks, and generally their lines do not interfere with divers, although it is a good idea to carry a knife to free oneself from lost fishing line.

The kelp bed east of Fish Rocks and between the rocks and the shore is very productive for seven-to eight-inch red abalone. Here the bottom consists of small boulders and some sand, and most of the abalone located in the cracks between the boulders. A large healthy bed of bull kelp covers the surface throughout the area, while palm kelp extends three to four feet above the bottom. Abalone divers are most successful when they can swim through the layer of palm kelp to find the abalone that hide below.

Many divers miss seeing much of the colorful invertebrate life as they search for game. Under the palm kelp exists a whole community that many never take the time to see. Many species of nudibranchs can be found here, including the clown nudibranch, the thick-horned aeolid, the white-lined dirona and the outrageous Spanish shawl. Many small featherduster worms, orange sea cucumbers, and numerous purple ringed top snails are also commonly found.

The area around Quinliven Rocks on the east side of the bay has a good population of abalone, and generally run bigger than around Fish Rocks, with some monster 9-to 10-inch abs taken here each year. Here one finds a sand bottom with rock pinnacles that jut up from the 20-to 30-foot bottom to near or above the surface. The abalone are found on the pinnacles just off of the sand or back in wide cracks. The fishing here, however, is poor.

The bay itself consists of a 20-to 30-foot rock and sand bottom and is generally not as interesting as the areas just west and east of the bay, with a few small abalone and fish being found here. An exception to this is the wash rock in the mouth of the bay where one finds colorful invertebrate life and an occasional lingcod.

Much of the diving at Anchor Bay is done from small, inflatable boats. Boats are easily launched during the summer months (mid June through mid November) when the beach is covered with sand. During winter and spring the currents change and wash away the sand, leaving a boulder- strewn beach from which boat launching is difficult. The center of the beach has a relatively unpredictable shore break, making it easy to flip an inflatable. For this reason most boats are launched on the western part of the beach, affectionately referred to as "chicken cove."

Anchor Bay offers first class game collecting areas, as well as beautiful underwater topography and marine life. This is a family campground and non-divers will find plenty to do beachcombing, exploring or just catching rays while the divers "bring home the bacon."

Access, Entry, and Hazards: Anchor Bay is just north of Gualala at MEN 4.64 and beach access is through the campground that is just north of the town. Restrooms, coin-op showers, a fish cleaning house, and fresh water are available at the campground. Small boats may be easily launched from the beach when the sand is in (mid June through mid November). For campground reservations or diving report, call 707-884-4222.

S.S. Crescent City

The *S.S. Crescent City* was built in San Francisco in 1882, and was a coal-burning, wooden-hulled steamer. She grossed 296 tons, was 145 feet long, 28 feet wide and drew 12 feet below the water line. This ship provided remarkably regular service between San Francisco and the port of Crescent City.

On Thursday afternoon January 29, 1903, Captain Payne and the *Crescent City* left San Francisco bound for Mendocino with 12 passengers and 16 crew. She also carried an assortment of light cargo that would have been shipped by rail, if one existed at that time. When the ship cleared Point Reyes the weather turned bad with a 60 mile per hour wind and rain. This was a southeasterly gale, typical of winter storms in California.

Captain Payne retired to his cabin about midnight and left the vessel in the hands of first mate Olesen. The crew figured that the ship was making her normal nine knots and miscalculated that the wind and swell was driving her a bit faster and a bit inshore. At 2 a.m. the passengers were tossed out of their bunks when the ship ran aground. The ship had entered the channel between Fish Rocks and the mainland, just north of Anchor Bay and finally came to rest in the lee of Fish Rocks. The hull stove in and the engine room flooded, making it unlikely that the ship would ever float again.

Captain Payne came quickly to the deck and took charge. The ship came to rest so close to the island that all the crew had to do is drop a plank and everyone safely walked ashore. A shelter was made for the women and children, but the men spent the night standing in the rain next to a fire of driftwood.

The Schooner *Scotia* spotted the wreck at 10 a.m. the following morning and sent her boat in to help. The passengers were ferried to near-by Iverson's Landing while the crew chose to remain with the ship, spending another night on Fish Rocks. On Saturday morning the tugboat *Relief* made it to the wreck site, and after ascertaining that the *Crescent City* was on the rocks for good, rescued the stranded crew. Everyone from the *Crescent City* was taken back to San Francisco on the *Relief*, except for three passengers who were in no hurry to get on another ship.

Before too long the waves began to break over the top of the wreck and the bow began to break up. The insurance company paid for a salvage attempt. The ship was filled with barrels and the rock blasted away from underneath the wreck to free her. The ship was only briefly afloat when another large wave came in, and lifted her back on the rocks. All attempts to refloat her were abandoned, and much of the machinery was subsequently removed from the wreck. The next storm lifted the wreck off the rocks and smashed her to bits against the mainland.

Artifact hunters should begin their search on the open-water side of Fish Rocks where the bottom begins in 20 feet of water and slopes to over 100 feet to a sand bottom. This area is highly textured with tall pinnacles, deep cracks and high-sided canyons. Although most of the shipwreck hit these rocks first, the wrecks were always lifted from the rocks and deposited on the mainland. There were so many ships wrecked here that it is difficult to determine which part came from which ship.

The kelp bed east of Fish Rocks and between the rocks and the shore is also a good place to find artifacts. Here the bottom consists of small boulders and some sand with a lot of abalone located in the cracks between the boulders. A large healthy bed of bull kelp covers the surface throughout the area, while palm kelp extends three to four feet above the bottom. Divers should part the palm kelp and fan the sand bottom to reveal artifacts.

Since most of the ships from the late 1800s early 1900s were made of wood it's not obvious what to look for. Much of the heavy machinery and engines were removed before the ships broke up, so divers will most often find small pieces of brass pipe, fittings and the rare porthole. Since much of the metal is now covered with marine growth, the artifacts look just like rocks. If you carry a small hammer or abalone iron with you, try tapping on the bottom. Metal on rock will make a dull thud, while metal on metal will make a ringing sound.

The best time to look for artifacts is during the winter months and early spring. In California the sand makes a seasonal migration, out in winter and back in the following spring. In the summer and fall the beach at Anchor bay is wide and covered with nice, fine sand. In winter there is no sand on the beach at all! It is not very productive to look for artifacts during summertime when they are covered with several feet of sand.

Divers may swim to good ab hunting grounds by walking to the eastern end of the beach and swimming 100 to 200 yards southeast to Quinliven Rocks. It is also a 200-yard swim to the wash rock in the center of the cove. To reach Fish Rocks, divers should be prepared for a long one-half mile swim each way. Those with the stamina and without a boat will find the effort worthwhile. Divers should, however, be observant of the weather as wind and surge can pick up quickly. In the summer months you will be swimming into the wind while heading to Fish Rocks and, with it, returning.

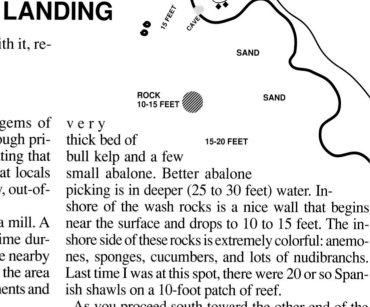

Collins Landing

Collins Landing is one of the hidden gems of Mendocino Dive sites. Public access is through private property, and there are no signs indicating that beach access is available. This is a spot that locals frequent, and where you will find few, if any, out-of-town divers.

Collins Landing had a small facility with a mill. A Mr. Collins operated for a short period of time during the late 1800s, but closed down when the nearby stands of redwoods were logged out. Today the area is populated by bed-and-breakfast establishments and rental houses.

The main cove has a rock and sand bottom with depths from 15 to 30 feet. You must swim 150 yards or more to reach depths much over 30 feet. There are a few small abalone in the cove, along with a few fish. The generally poor visibility and lack of game sends divers to the point at the north end of the cove. Here divers find plentiful abalone in 20 to 25 feet of water, along with some rockfish. The bottom here consists of large boulders on a sand bottom. Anemones, urchins and sponges cling tenaciously to the rocky bottom.

Better diving may be found to the little cove to the south of the entry point. The water is often substantially clearer than the north cove and it's a shorter swim. After you enter the water, just head left (south) and swim between the large offshore rocks. The area just south of the rocks is a snorkeler's paradise. There are more species of kelp here than I have ever seen in one place. The numerous species of kelp, along with their bizarre shapes and colors, make this one of the best snorkeling spots on the North Coast—all in two to four feet of water.

As one proceeds southwest the depth gradually drops to 10 to 15 feet. The bottom here is rock with boulders scattered about. The rocky bottom supports a very thick bed of bull kelp and a few small abalone. Better abalone picking is in deeper (25 to 30 feet) water. Inshore of the wash rocks is a nice wall that begins near the surface and drops to 10 to 15 feet. The inshore side of these rocks is extremely colorful: anemones, sponges, cucumbers, and lots of nudibranchs. Last time I was at this spot, there were 20 or so Spanish shawls on a 10-foot patch of reef.

As you proceed south toward the other end of the cove the bottom becomes mostly sand, with rocky patch reefs sprinkled about. There are some abalone here but the diving is interesting until you get a little further from shore. About 200 yards from the beach is a nice little rocky patch with a lot of invertebrates and a fair amount of fish. The abalone diving on this rock is spectacular. There are abalone piled on top of each other, some of them are a very respectable size. This is a good spot for beginners since the rock is not much more than fifteen feet deep.

Access, Entry and Hazards: At MEN 3.83 turn west into the Serenisea Lodge facilities. Park in one of the few public parking spaces at the west end of the traffic circle. Follow the public access path that begins to the right of the office and proceeds behind the office and follow a steep, well-maintained stairway to the beach. Enter off the small gravel beach to the left. There are cabins for rent, but there are no facilities for day users. Call Serenisea Lodge at 707-884-3836, 800-331-3836, or www.serenisea.com. You may also park at MEN 4.00 and hike to the point north of the cove and down the cliff. Watch for big surge and swell.

Metridium anemone.

Introduction to Sonoma County

The 30-mile stretch of coastline between the Gualala River and the Russian River is certainly the most heavily dived in all of Northern California. Divers flock here because of the numerous and well-protected entries, abundance of game, and proximity to the bay area. It is possible to drive to Sonoma County from San Francisco, blow a tank, pop a limit of abalone and be back in The City in time for dinner. Many of the dive sites described in this section have entries that beginners can handle and advanced divers will enjoy as well. You will find "diver friendly" accommodations throughout the county.

The northern portion of Sonoma County is occupied by The Sea Ranch. This private community limits public access to the beach; however, seven trailheads have been established for public access. These fee lots have limited parking, but offer access to good abalone hunting grounds and excellent topside scenery. Visibility here is often poor, but due to the limited access, game hunting is excellent.

South of The Sea Ranch is a large stretch of beautiful coastline and fine diving. However, the area is privately owned and there is no public access. The situation changes south of Stewards Point where a series of state and county parks and privately held campgrounds provide convenient access to great diving. Salt Point State Park stands out as the premier dive spot in this area, mainly due to the marine reserve at Gerstle Cove. South of Salt Point to Fort Ross are several sheltered coves with good diver access, campgrounds, motels, and facilities to launch boats.

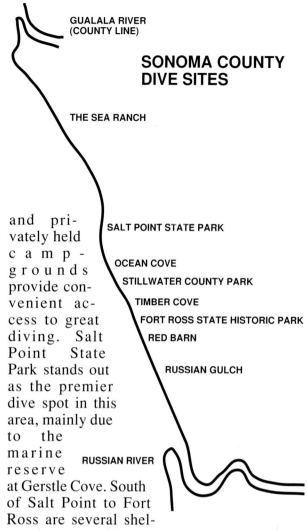

SONOMA COUNTY DIVE SITES

GUALALA RIVER (COUNTY LINE)

THE SEA RANCH

SALT POINT STATE PARK

OCEAN COVE

STILLWATER COUNTY PARK

TIMBER COVE

FORT ROSS STATE HISTORIC PARK

RED BARN

RUSSIAN GULCH

RUSSIAN RIVER

The coastline, South of Fort Ross State Historic Park to Jenner, presents divers with steep cliffs, bad visibility, and good abalone diving. Those who are part mountain goat will enjoy the exercise of hiking, with all their gear, down and up the area's steep and long trails. Hey, everyone has a right to do what feels good.

South of Jenner to the County Line lie a series of county-owned beaches with easy access but lousy diving. The generally sand bottom coupled with the outfall from the nearby Russian River does not make for good dive spots. You would be better off driving another 15 minutes north to vastly superior sites.

In addition to the campgrounds and motels listed with each dive site there are numerous rental homes available throughout Sonoma County. Call Bodega Bay & Beyond at 800-888-3565, or 707-875-3942, or on the web at "www.sonomacoast.com."

Diver with hydrocoral.

The Sea Ranch

The land south of the Gualala River was once covered by thick redwood forests. Intensive logging began during the 1860s and continued through the early 1900s, and at least four landings operated off and on, along with their associated mills. The area later became a cattle ranch and farm. 1962 developers began to create an upscale, second home community. For a while the Sea Ranch jealously guarded its privacy and no trespassing signs kept divers from these pristine reefs.

Then in 1987 the California Coastal Commission directed Sonoma County to establish and maintain seven public, coastal access points throughout this community. Parking areas were built between two-tenths and six-tenths miles from the beach, and 15-foot wide, well-maintained trails with stairways were constructed. Because of previous limited access this is an excellent spot for ab diving. With minimal effort divers should expect to find large, plentiful abalone in 10 to 15 feet of water in the kelp beds right offshore. Little tank diving is done here because of the long walk to the beach and divers should avoid this area on rough days as it is very exposed. All of these beaches are ideal spots for picnicking, for a game of frisbee, or an after-dive nap.

Typical of Sea Ranch Diving is Pebble Beach. This site may be reached via a three-tenths mile trail beginning at SON 52.29. This beach is moderately protected from the northwesterlies, and good diving may be found a short swim from shore. Most divers head to the north point to dive in 10 to 30 feet of water. The bottom here is rock and sand with a thin covering of bull kelp. In some areas the rocks jut straight up from the sand, creating a series of mini-walls. On top of the rocks is a rag mop covering of coralline algae. Farther down the walls is a colorful collection of encrusting sponges and anemones. Shy shrimp and tiny fish hide among the nooks-and-crannies of the rocks. Look for an assortment of gaudy nudibranchs wandering across the sponges or feeding on hydroids.

It is not the color that draws divers here but the abalone. Like buttons running down a shirt, the abalone are located at the boundary between the rock and sand. These are in plain view and are easy to spot, even for beginners.

In other areas the rock barely rises above the sandy bottom. Here the predominant life is palm kelp. This kelp grows on short stalks with the fronds some three feet off the bottom. Here the abalone are sprinkled randomly on flat rocks. Abs here are not as plentiful as in the more textured areas, and divers must part the layer of palm kelp to find the animals that lurk beneath.

Another access point to the beach is at the end of Whaler's Reach. Divers hike along a cypress tree-covered path to the ocean. The walk to the water is half the fun, since the vegetation creates a completely covered walkway that all but blots out the sun. The covered path ends at a rocky point, from which are many routes to the water. Some entries are an easy scamper down a rocky ramp to the sea, while others involve a bit of a climb down a short, but steep cliff. Which entry you choose should depend upon the direction and size of the swell, as well as your climbing and diving skills. Offshore you will find a rock and sand bottom and a thin bed of bull kelp.

This entry may only be used by landowners and their guests, and that means this spot is better for game hunting than the northern side of the beach. Abalone are bigger and more plentiful, and there are more fish as well. Lingcod are commonly found hiding back in deep cracks while cabezon are seen perched on a rock waiting for a crab to wander by. Look for blue rockfish on the outside of the kelp beds.

The most northerly of the Sea Ranch public access points is the Walk On Beach parking lot located at SON 56.53. The trail to the beach is four-tenths miles long and leads to a little cove. This is a great place for beachcombing and picnicking. However, due to the proximity of the Gualala River the visibility is often poor, although there a few abalone here.

A better place to hunt for both abalone and fish is

THE SEA RANCH

HWY. 1

DEL MAR LANDING ECOLOGICAL RESERVE

TRAIL HEAD

TRAIL HEAD

WALK ON BEACH

SHELL BEACH

TRAIL HEAD

TRAIL HEAD

STENGEL BEACH

HWY. 1

PEBBLE BEACH

TRAIL HEAD

BLACK POINT BEACH

BLACK POINT

SS Klamath

The *Klamath* was a 662-ton wooden steamer that had accomodations for 75 passengers. She mainly paid her way by hauling lumber down the coast and light freight up the coasts. On February 4, 1921 Captain Thomas Jamieson, 19 passengers, and 34 crew headed north out of San Francisco for Portland. Late that evening the wind came up and the boat ran into the full force of a hurricane with 70- to 100-mile per hour winds. The wind swept the *Klamath* shoreward and tossed her like a piece of driftwood. She finally came to shore at 2 a.m. on February 5th, about one-half mile south of Del Mar Landing and about one mile north of the point where the Walk On Beach trail hits the beach. Miraculously, all of the passengers and crew made it safely to shore. Later the next day the crew was able to salvage all of the passenger's luggage before she broke up in the swell. There is not much left of the ship today, but abalone divers occasionally find a piece of brass or iron engine parts.

Shell Beach (SON 55.24). The six-tenths mile trail leads to a gravel beach with a wide access road. Small inflatable boats and dive kayaks may be launched here if they are light enough to be hand carried, and you have a right to private access. The boat-friendly access is not for public use. This is where the Sonoma County Sheriffs Department launch their boats on rough days. Offshore are a series of rocky reefs with lots of abalone and fish. The invertebrate population here is also good for sightseers and photographers.

The Stengel Beach (SON 53.96) trailhead and parking lot is the starting point for a short (two-tenths mile) trail to a pretty beach with a waterfall that drops directly onto the beach. There are a few abalone here but the bottom is mostly sand. This is a great place for picnicking and surfing when the waves are up.

Black Point Beach (SON 50.85) may be reached after a short, three-tenths mile hike that winds down a set of stairs. This long sandy beach is a great place for a picnic during the summer months. However, it is northwest facing and the predominant northwesterly summer swell often makes this site undivable. On calm days or when a southerly swell is running, this a great place to dive for abalone or

Sea Ranch.

to spearfish. Enter the water near the stairs and swim around the point to your left. There are many abalone in the eight-to nine-inch range, with some good potential for spearfishing.

Access, Entry, and Hazards: Each public trailhead has limited parking, a telephone, and a restroom. The wide trails are well-maintained and there is a fee for parking. This is an honor system and the county asks that you place the parking fee with vehicle information in the obvious receptacle. Little tank diving is done here because of the long walk to the beach. There are no public facilities outside of the public trailheads. This part of the coast is less protected than other areas and divers should watch for big surf and surge. There may be a longshore current should you swim out past the kelp.

All but one of the sites described above allow public access. If you are renting a house at the Sea Ranch, you may dive anywhere it is safe and where you do not trespass. There are numerous small parking lots throughout the community where home owners and their guests may park. Please respect the privacy of homeowners. My favorite areas are to the north and south of Shell Beach, and between Stingel Beach and Pebble Beach. There are a great many access points along this stretch of coastline. So pick your entry carefully and enjoy the rocky bottom with plenty of abalone. Be sure to watch the ocean for a while before entering as the swell here can be dangerous. However, there are many safe places to enter and the area offers some trophy abalone in the 10-inch+ range and some great spearfishing. On calm days you may also want to bring your camera along for some great macro photography. There is a reserve in the northern portion of the community where no marine life may be taken.

For vacation house rentals, call Rams Head Realty and Rentals, Inc. at 707-785-2427 or Sea Ranch Vacation Homes at 707-884-4235.

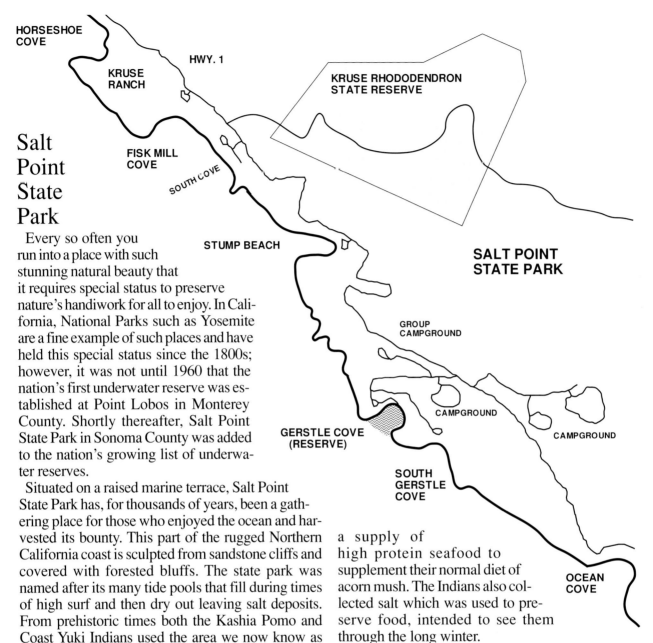

HORSESHOE COVE

KRUSE RANCH

HWY. 1

KRUSE RHODODENDRON STATE RESERVE

FISK MILL COVE

SOUTH COVE

STUMP BEACH

SALT POINT STATE PARK

GROUP CAMPGROUND

CAMPGROUND

CAMPGROUND

GERSTLE COVE (RESERVE)

SOUTH GERSTLE COVE

OCEAN COVE

Salt Point State Park

Every so often you run into a place with such stunning natural beauty that it requires special status to preserve nature's handiwork for all to enjoy. In California, National Parks such as Yosemite are a fine example of such places and have held this special status since the 1800s; however, it was not until 1960 that the nation's first underwater reserve was established at Point Lobos in Monterey County. Shortly thereafter, Salt Point State Park in Sonoma County was added to the nation's growing list of underwater reserves.

Situated on a raised marine terrace, Salt Point State Park has, for thousands of years, been a gathering place for those who enjoyed the ocean and harvested its bounty. This part of the rugged Northern California coast is sculpted from sandstone cliffs and covered with forested bluffs. The state park was named after its many tide pools that fill during times of high surf and then dry out leaving salt deposits. From prehistoric times both the Kashia Pomo and Coast Yuki Indians used the area we now know as Salt Point as their summer home. They didn't come here to tan on the area's beaches, but rather to harvest

a supply of high protein seafood to supplement their normal diet of acorn mush. The Indians also collected salt which was used to preserve food, intended to see them through the long winter.

The first white man to occupy the land was a German named William Rufus who ran a cattle ranch. A mill was established in 1853 at Gerstle's Cove, but the dog hole port and landing always went by the name Salt Point. The gulches were logged back as far as oxen could haul logs, and a quarry thrived for a short time as well. The owners moved the saw mill to the Russian River in 1860 and the landing fell out of use.

About the same time, William Miller had logged out Timber Cove and decided to move his operation to one of the coves north of Salt Point, probably at the old, abandoned Fisk's Mill. A railroad was put in and a small town sprung up around the mill. The post office at Timber Cove even moved to Salt Point. The town was named Louisville and, for a short while,

Diver with red octopus.

had the largest hotel in Sonoma County, all six rooms worth. The timber was logged out in 1876 and Miller moved his mill to Rockport. Louisville then dried up and the post office moved back to Timber Cove. In the 1890s the ranch was bought up by an Irishman named Walsh. It was his descendants who sold the land to the state of California.

Many only visit Salt Point State Park to dive, and end up missing much of what the park has to offer. Many miles of hiking trails lead along wind and wave sculptured sandstone bluffs, through wildflower covered meadows, and redwood forests. Kruze Rhododendron State Reserve is adjacent to the park, and in the spring the pink blossoms of the rhododendron add color to the redwood canopy above.

The park has two campgrounds in addition to a group campground. For recorded diving conditions, call 707-847-3222. For additional information call 707-847-3221. Reservations may be made by calling 800-444-PARK. The Salt Point Lodge is located just south of the park and has reasonably priced rooms and a hot tub and sauna, as well as an excellent restaurant. Call 707-847-3234 for reservations.

Horseshoe Cove

The bottom of this north-facing cove is gravel with small boulders. Many divers only visit this spot when conditions at other sites are blown out. The walk to the beach is short, but very steep, and a few divers occasionally haul tanks down the cliff. The bottom of the cove is coarse gravel with boulders. Abalone and game are mostly absent. Small abalone may be found deep in cracks along the protected lip of the cove directly across the cove from where the trail hits the beach. Depths in the cove and along the wall very between 10 to 15 feet.

The bottom off the south point of the cove is rocky with large boulders. Depths run between 30 and 60 feet and there are plenty of abalone and fish. This is a

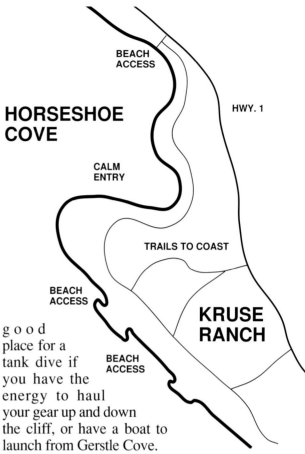

good place for a tank dive if you have the energy to haul your gear up and down the cliff, or have a boat to launch from Gerstle Cove.

Access, Entry and Hazards: Park at the turnout along Highway 1 at SON 44.23. Hike along the trail that proceeds west from the turnout and down the steep bluff to the gravel beach. Alternatively, divers can follow a trail around to the south of the cove and down the well-marked and more gently graded slope to the beach. This is a calm entry when a south wind and swell are running, but can get rough when the northwesterlies are blowing. Enter in the protection of the point and swim around to the left and south. There are no facilities.

Kruse Ranch

The Kruse Ranch area offers some of the finest near-shore diving in the county. The rugged shoreline is sculpted by wind and waves into an artful display of arches, caves, canyons and textured surfaces. The beautiful scenery extends underwater to a mostly rock bottom. Coralline and red algae cover many of the near-shore rocks to about 20 feet. The textured bottom offers plenty of shelter for abalone, rockfish and lingcod. There are a fair number of abalone here, but no monsters.

In deeper water the bottom is even more impressive with large rocks and cracks, rocky outcroppings and swim throughs. Large anemones and colorful sponges

Diver with lingcod.

add color to the scenery and game hunting gets better as you move offshore towards reefs that are 60 feet deep.

Access, Entry and Hazards: Park at one of the turnouts at SON 44.00, 43.90, or 43.66. There are many trails to the ocean. All are long but not very steep. Once you arrive at the bluffs there are numerous ways to scamper/climb a short distance to many entry spots. Choose yours based on the size and direction of swell, as well as your climbing and diving abilities. This part of the coast is exposed to prevailing weather and offers little protection. Dive here on only the calmest of days. There are no facilities.

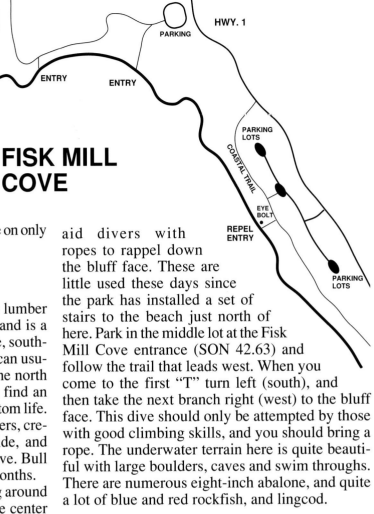

Fisk Mill Cove

Fisk Mill Cove takes its name from the lumber mill that operated here in the late 1800s, and is a recent addition to the state park. This large, south-facing cove can be very rough, but divers can usually enter the water on the south side of the north point when the swell is up. Here one can find an abundance of abalone with some pretty bottom life. The bottom is covered with massive boulders, creating numerous cracks for abalone to hide, and varies between 10 to 30 feet within the cove. Bull and palm kelp may be thick in summer months.

Better diving may be found by swimming around to the north side of the point or within the center of the cove. The bottom consists of rock bottom that gently slopes out to 60 to 70 feet. Numerous rocky ridges and rock piles dot the bottom a short distance from shore, where a large population of abalone and fish may be found. This is one of the best spearfishing spots in Sonoma and large lingcod, cabezon, and vermilion rockfish are frequently found here.

Access, Entry and Hazards: Divers may park in the well-marked park entrance at SON 42.63, pay a fee, and park in the most northerly of the paved lots. They can then follow the trail north to the bluff face and down a set of wooden stairs. Alternatively, divers may park in the free, dirt lot on the west side of the road at SON 43.06, follow the trails across the bluff, and scramble down bluff or take the wooden staircase to a rocky beach. Alternatively, you may take the longer trail on the right to the rocky point. There is a restroom in the paved parking area.

At one spot near the southern portion of the cove several eye-bolts have been placed in the rock to aid divers with ropes to rappel down the bluff face. These are little used these days since the park has installed a set of stairs to the beach just north of here. Park in the middle lot at the Fisk Mill Cove entrance (SON 42.63) and follow the trail that leads west. When you come to the first "T" turn left (south), and then take the next branch right (west) to the bluff face. This dive should only be attempted by those with good climbing skills, and you should bring a rope. The underwater terrain here is quite beautiful with large boulders, caves and swim throughs. There are numerous eight-inch abalone, and quite a lot of blue and red rockfish, and lingcod.

South Cove

South Cove is south of Fisk Mill Cove. This little beach is moderately protected from swell by a rocky point and an offshore reef. The area inshore of a line drawn north of the point is shallow (10 to 15 feet) and is rocky with jumbles of large boulders. There are fair numbers of small (seven to eight inch) abalone here. Should you venture past the reef into deeper water (30 to 40 feet) you will find a nicely textured rock and sand bottom with numerous large (eight and a half to nine and a half inch) abalone and some game fish. This area is pretty with colorful sponges and anemones dotting the rocky walls.

Access, Entry and Hazards: Divers should park at a little turnout on the west side of Highway 1 at SON 42.36, and follow the trail to the bluff and out and down a point of land. Follow the trail to the inshore side of the rocky point to the beach. Watch for big surf and swell. There are no facilities.

Stump Beach

Stump Beach is a great place to leave your tanks behind and experience the joy of breath-hold diving. Because the trail is so long and so steep, most divers choose to free-dive here. Stump Beach is wide with fine sand and is more reminiscent of Southern California than the predominantly rocky coastline of the north. The cove is deeply inset and very picturesque. When viewed from above, the cove often takes on a deep emerald green color under a noonday sun.

The inshore portions of the cove are much like the beach, very sandy. Perhaps, there were once a few abalone along the rocky walls of the cove, but have been taken a long time ago. To get to good diving you must swim or paddle to the cove's mouth. It is a long swim to open water, about one-quarter mile, so many divers bring kayaks or at least surf mats along to make the swim easier.

Good abalone hunting and spearfishing may be found in the rocky area, just outside and north of the cove. Here the bottom is mostly rock with large boulders, some 15 to 30 feet deep. A thick layer of bull kelp covers the surface in summer months, and another layer of palm kelp sways about three feet off the bottom. Abalone are found underneath this layer of palm kelp or upside down beneath larger rocks.

There is also plenty of fish and invertebrate life here. Colorful nudibranchs are commonplace, and there is a varied assortment of crabs, shrimp, anemones and other critters. This is also a good spot to seek out game fish such as lingcod, cabezon, and various rockfish.

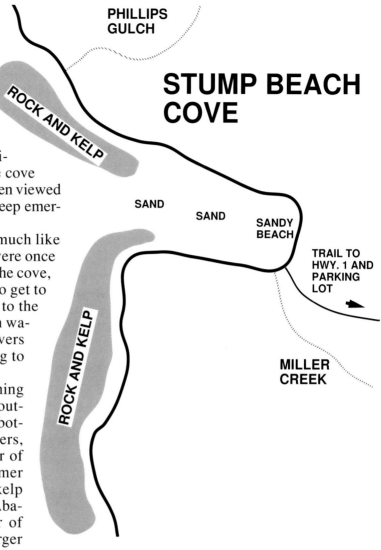

Divers exit the water at Stump Beach.

Access, Entry and Hazards: Divers heading north on Highway 1 should park in the well-marked lot at SON 41.22, about two and one-half miles north of the Salt Point State Park entrance. Next to the parking area is a picnic area that is situated among a grove of redwoods and has a great view of the ocean and cove. Divers then may follow the one-quarter mile trail that heads out from the parking area and switchbacks down to the beach. There is a restroom in the picnic area.

This cove can get very rough as it faces directly into the summer, northwest swell. When the wave action is low or if a southern swell is running, the cove can be glassy and then it is a popular spot for beginning scuba classes. When the surf is up it is better to pick a more protected entry such as Gerstle Cove or Fisk Mill Cove. Watch for rip currents in the center of the cove.

Gerstle Cove

Although Salt Point State Park has numerous good diving areas, Gerstle Cove has become synonymous with Salt Point diving. The cove itself is a marine reserve in which no marine life may be taken or disturbed. This is an excellent place to observe and photograph underwater life since examples of most all of the north coasts species may be found here. Ten-inch red abalone may be seen here along with rock scallops and large game fish. Because of the area's reserve status these animals grow to large sizes in the absence of human predation.

Gerstle Cove has a rugged, rock bottom consisting of large and small boulders and a small amount of sand between the rocks. Depths range from 10 to 30 feet within the reserve. Within the reserve is a profusion of life. Several species of anemone including the bright red, rose and the giant green anemone dot the bottom. Colorful orange sea cucumbers are common and some rocks are covered with red sea stars and bat stars. Several species of nudibranchs are common, including the yellow-edged cadlina and the thick-horned aeolid. Palm kelp stands three to four feet from the bottom in both shallow and deeper areas, while bull kelp forms a canopy over the deeper areas.

The bottom outside of the reserve is more barren

Map labels:
GROUP CAMPGROUND
HWY. 1
SALT POINT STATE PARK
PARKING
BARN
PARKING
20 FEET
RESERVE
MOONROCK CAMPGROUND
SALT POINT
30 FEET
GERSTLE COVE
SOUTH GERSTLE COVE PICNIC AREA

Bat ray.

SS Norlina

The *SS Norlina* was 383 feet long, 51 feet wide and had a 26-foot-deep cargo hold. She was originally christened the *Georgiana* in 1909 and after several name changes she was purchased by the Garland Line. She was renamed *Norlina* and was put her into inter-coastal trade, a job that took her through the Panama Canal on many occasions.

On July 31, 1926 she landed in San Francisco for a routine stop. Most of the freight was unloaded in San Francisco, and what remained was mainly general cargo-nails, bolts and the like. At 5 p.m. on August 3, she headed up the coast for her next regular stop in Seattle. By 10 p.m. they had rounded Point Reyes and the captain turned in for the night. Most of the crew, along with the captain, had spent much of the evening bar hopping along the San Francisco waterfront and had a few too many.

Around 1 a.m. the next morning the ship ran into a thick fog bank and the second mate tried to roust the captain for new orders. After several failed attempts to wake the Captain he went back to the bridge and continued north at full speed.

About 2:30 a.m. the mate heard a grating noise and the *Norlina* shuddered to a halt. They had run aground on the rocks just south of Salt Point, and their momentum carried them about one-third the length of the ship onto the rocks, and ripped a gash in the bow and down the keel. The hold began to fill with water.

The crew radioed for help and the tug *Sea Salvor* and the Coast Guard Cutter *Shawnee* were dispatched. Both arrived around 5 p.m., but had to stand off until the next day due to the high seas. By this time the *Norlina* was listing badly and the engine room had filled with water.

The crew was safely pulled off by the *Shawnee* and brought back to San Francisco for questioning. During the hearing one of the crew claimed the captain was no good and was drunk the night of the shipwreck. Afterwards two of the crew, still loyal to the captain, jumped the man and beat him from head to foot, knocking out six teeth. In the end the captain and second mate pleaded guilty to negligence and the inquiry board suspended their licenses for a few months.

Some of the cargo, the anchors and a few good winches were later pulled off the ship. A salvage company tired to refloat her, but she sank as soon as they got her off the rocks. Remains of the steel plates and pipe fittings may still be found outside the south side of Little Gerstle Cove.

---

than within, and has a 30-foot flat, rock bottom that slopes down to 90 feet. Abalone hunting here for 7- to 8-inch specimens is fair in 25 to 30 feet of water, as the flat bottom offers little shelter for protection. In a little deeper water fair spearfishing for lingcod, cabezon and rockfish may be found. Large bat rays are sometimes found in the far side of the kelp beds. Make sure that you are well outside of the reserve before taking game.

Hermissenda nudibranch.

The best abalone diving in the area is off of the rocks on the north side of Salt Point. Park near the entrance of the Gerstle Cove Parking lot and hike the short distance to the rocky beach. Be very careful about entries and exits here. This point is very exposed to waves and swell; conditions can change rapidly, making it diveable only on calm days. A dense population of 8-inch abalone may be found in 15 to 30 feet of water. This area also has some very pretty underwater topography with large rocks, overhangs, and an abundance of colorful anemones and sponges.

Access, Entry and Hazards: Turn west from Highway 1 at SON 39.89, pay a fee at the kiosk, and follow the sights to the beach. Park in the large lot on the bluff. A paved road leads to Gerstle Cove. Small inflatables and kayaks may be launched here and there is a restroom, cold showers, and a fish cleaning station above the cove. Painted wooden posts at each side of the cove mark the reserve boundaries. Make sure you are well outside of the reserve before taking game as all marine life is protected within the reserve. Watch for thick kelp, big waves and surge, and boat traffic.

South Gerstle Cove

Just south of the reserve parking lot is another lot with a dirt trail that leads down the bluff to South Gerstle Cove. Here is a small, rocky beach that is somewhat exposed to the prevailing swell. Freedivers can find a good population of seven-to eight-inch abalone after a short swim to either the north or south side of the outer part of the cove. Those who are willing to haul tanks down the 40-foot bluff face will find a colorful, rocky bottom with some good spearfishing in 40 to 50 feet of water outside of the cove.

Access, Entry, and Hazards: Follow the directions to Gerstle Cove. Before you enter the Gerstle Cove parking area, turn left and follow the road that ends in the South Gerstle parking lot. Follow the trail across the bluff and down to the rocky beach. Watch for thick kelp and big waves and surge.

Ocean Cove

Ocean Cove is located just south of Salt Point State Park and was once known as Walsh's Landing. The Walsh family operated a mill and landing here and at one time owned much of the land that is currently Salt Point State Park. Today the cove and surrounding land is privately owned. The owners operate a campground and store, and offer access to divers and other ocean enthusiasts.

Ocean Cove is well protected and provides comfortable access to the ocean, particularly for those with boats or kayaks. A dirt road runs between Highway 1 and the beach, making this a very convenient place to launch inflatable boats or kayaks to explore remote dive sites or for easy access to the cove.

The bottom of Ocean Cove is mostly rock, sprinkled with boulders. Coralline algae covers many of the inshore rocks and palm kelp covers the bottom in waters that are a bit deeper. The area supports a healthy population of abalone. Abalone in the cove may be hard to find, but if the surf is up divers can still find their limit along the south and north sides of the cove. The cove and adjacent reefs support a thick growth of bull kelp. The latter is convenient since bull kelp is one of the red abalone's favorite food. The rocky bottom and abundant food supply make for a productive abalone fishery.

Beach divers will find good diving at Ocean Cove. Many drive to the bluff's edge near the southern point of the cove and scampering down the 20-foot bluff. Plentiful, legal-sized abalone are found near shore and in only 10 to 15 feet of water. The sometimes surgy environment and thick cover of bull and palm kelp make it a bit challenging to find your limit, but the inshore fish and invertebrate life make this a worthwhile experience.

A bit farther offshore divers will find a 20-to 30-foot rock bottom with more and bigger (8 to 8 1/2 inches) abalone. The bottom here is composed of large rocks and boulders and offers a good environment where fish and abalone can hide. Look back in cracks and under ledges for your abalone, particularly the big ones. Don't forget to look for lingcod back in the ledges as well. When the ocean is calm, you'll want to explore reefs outside of the main cove, particularly if you have a boat.

Access, Entry, and Hazards: Enter the area through the Ocean Cove Campground at SON 38.00. There is a fee for camping, day use, boat and kayak launching, and there is a general store with some dive equipment and an air station on weekends (April through November). Reservations are accepted only for group camping, call 707-847-3422. Chemical toilets and hot showers are available. Divers may follow the unpaved road to the rocky beach or enter off the southern point of the cove. Watch for big waves and surge along with boat traffic.

Salt Point Lodge overlooks the cove and has good rooms (some with private fireplaces and hot tubs), a community hot tub and sauna, and a very good restaurant. Call 707-847-3234 for reservations.

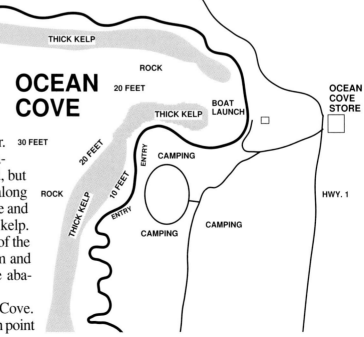

The Cauldron

This site is also known as the Washing Machine, and lies about 100 yards offshore in a shallow area bordered by a set of guardian wash rocks. The bowl-shaped area takes its name from the boiling cauldron appearance of the water when the surf is up, and is one of the best shallow-water abalone grounds on the north coast. Here, on a calm day, even beginner abalone divers may find 8-to 8 1/2-inch abalone in 10 to 15 feet of water. The area is covered with palm kelp and sometimes takes a bit of looking, but the population of legal sized red abalone here is quite large. The area just south of the rocks has a good population of 8-inch abalone in 25 to 40 feet of water, but few fish. The bottom is dotted with red, fish eating anemones in deeper water, and the giant green anemone in the shallows. This is a colorful area that is great for macro photography.

Access, Entry and Hazards: Park at the little turnout on Highway 1 at SON 37.52. There is a moderate hike down on a trail through a stream bed to a protected beach. It is a one-third mile swim each way to the Cauldron from Stillwater Cove, and some instructors have their classes swim there for exercise. An inflatable boat or kayak out of Stillwater or Ocean Cove is a better way of getting there. Most divers, however, hike down the from the bluff.

On calm days this is an excellent place to dive, but the area gets quite rough when the waves pick up. The conditions here can change rapidly, so divers who hike down the trail should be prepared to swim into Stillwater Cove if the swell picks up enough to make the nearer exit unsafe. Once divers leave the immediate area of the Cauldron they enter fairly deep water for a long swim, but one without fear from large breakers, all the way back to Stillwater.

Stillwater Cove

Just south of the Cauldron is Stillwater Cove. This area was once the site of a boy's school. In 1935 an advertisement for the school stated that for $225 they would take in your boy for two months. He would be housed and fed, taught to fish, hunt, ride horses, and given academic lessons as well. A perspective client also had the assurance of the owners of the ranch who, ". . . wished that (your boy) might learn some of agriculture's interesting lessons of plant and animal life. . . and the dignity of skill in the use of their own hands."

The price at that time included transportation by sea from either San Francisco or Los Angeles. One of the highlights of the trip was that the boys would sail under the much talked about Golden Gate Bridge, at that time still under construction. During its 40-year history, the Stillwater Cove Ranch for Boys facilitated the passage into manhood of many young Californians.

The founders of the school showed much wisdom in selecting the site for their school as it sits on a bluff above one of the most scenic parts of the Sonoma County coast and overlooks a very picturesque cove. The cove was not always called by the name Stillwater. Originally, it was known as Stockhoff's Cove after the rancher who first homesteaded there. The original Stillwater Cove was located a little north of present day Timber

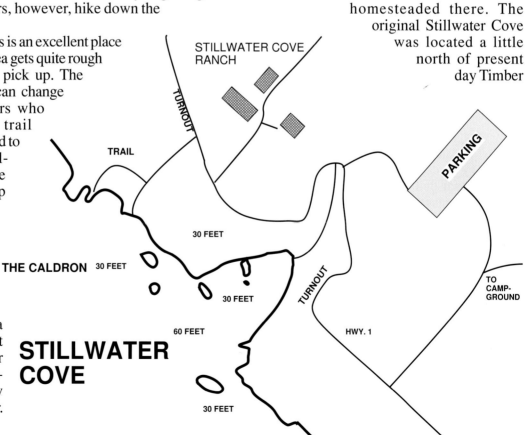

cove and was a dog hole port. When this dog hole closed, the owners of the boy's school "borrowed" the name Stillwater for their cove, and after a little while everyone forgot that there was an "another" Stillwater Cove.

Today, Stillwater Cove is a mecca for divers all around Northern California, and is known for its calm entries and excellent diving. The U-shaped cove faces southwest, providing ample protection from the dominant northwesterly swell. The ease of entry makes this a popular spot for scuba and free diving instructors to bring their beginner classes. For advanced divers Stillwater is a great place to launch a boat, kayak, or even swim to many sites for excellent game diving and photography.

The center of the cove consists of a highly textured boulder field with a few abalone of legal size, a bit of kelp, and is otherwise fairly barren. Out from the beach stretches a kelp bed consisting of mostly bull kelp , but a little giant and palm kelp can be found as well. Harbor seals are often found hauled out on the wash rocks north the cove.

The north and south walls of the cove are covered with an interesting collection of invertebrate life. Under a layers of coralline algae and sea lettuce may be found juvenile red abalone, red crabs, and an assortment of nudibranchs, including the sea lemon and the orange and white clown nudibranch. For beginners and macro-photographers this area can be interesting, but intermediate and advanced divers will find that the better diving is outside of the cove.

Straight out from the cove is an extensive bed of bull kelp under which is a series of rocky ridges and small holes in 40 to 60 feet of water. This is a good area to hunt for lingcod, cabezon, as well as blue and vermilion rockfish. It is particularly good for spearfishing in the late fall and winter when the large lingcod come out of deep water to mate and lay eggs.

Out from the far edge of the kelp runs a rock wall. The face runs along for about 200 feet and juts straight up 30 feet or so from a 80-to 90-foot bottom. Some call this rock, "The White Wall" because it is covered with Metridium anemones. On a clear day when the visibility is good enough to see even 20 percent of the length of the wall, the scale and beauty of this reef is nothing short of spectacular and puts many tropical reefs to shame. Hiding among the anemones are a selection of lingcod and cabezon, along with an assortment of crabs and nudibranchs. The Metridium, kelp canopy, and textured bottom make this an excellent place for wide-angle photography.

Clown nudibranch.

South of the Cove is an extensive boulder field that stretches out past a series of prominent wash rocks. This is an interesting place to explore on scuba because of the rugged bottom topography. There are many holes and a few small caves that are homes for a healthy assortment of rockfish and cabezon. Around the wash rock in 25 to 30 feet of water can be found a many abalone in the 8-to 9-inch range. Abalone may also be found in abundance between the wash rock and the south point of the cove, but you will have to be able to free-dive 30 to 40 feet to get at them. Conditions here can be very rough and caution is advised when the northwesterly swell in running.

Access, Entry, and Hazards: Stillwater Cove is run by Sonoma County as part of the Regional Park System. There is no parking at the cove, but there is a drop-off area 200 feet from the beach between SON 37.17 and 37.31. Proceed east at the intersection just south of the cove to the large day use parking lot, and follow the stairs to Highway 1 and the trail to the beach. Cars are not allowed on the paved path between the drop-off site and the beach, so if you have an inflatable boat it is best to have wheels for it. Day use parking is available in the lot on the hill above the cove (fee) or in the turnouts on the north and south sides of the cove (free). The park rangers discourage divers from parking in the turnouts as one must walk on the road to get back to the beach.

Divers should watch for boat traffic within the cove and big waves and surge at the exposed points of the cove. There are restrooms at the beach and campsites with showers (no reservations, first-come, first-serve) are available in the Park. For information, call 707-847-3245. There is a telephone in the upper parking lot.

You can also stay at the old boys' school, now called Stillwater Cove Ranch, call 707-847-3227. They no longer give riding and fishing lessons, but you can sleep in the old cook's house or in the "cow barn," now redecorated to handle guests. This is a charming place to stay in a rustic setting. History buffs will enjoy looking through a selection of photographs and documents from the old school.

Cemetery Reef

There are many offshore reefs along the Sonoma Coast. The most well known and typical of offshore reefs is Cemetery Reef. This reef is about half way between the south point of Stillwater Cove and the north point of Timber Cove. The top of the reef is in 20 to 30 feet of water and the sides drop nearly vertically to 50 feet and deeper.

The top of the reef is covered with bull and palm kelp. There are plenty of 8-to 8 1/2-inch abalone around if you can dive to 30 feet. As one gets a bit deeper the rocks are covered with Corynactis anemones, large Metridium anemones, barnacles and encrusting sponges. This area is pretty with lots of color for macro and wide-angle photography.

The rock walls drop to a jumble of huge boulders and rocks. There are abalone here, but well out of the range of free-divers. Look for large lingcod, cabezon, and vermilion rockfish among the nooks and crannies of the boulder field. Often large schools of blue rockfish may be found just offshore of the reef.

Access, Entry, and Hazards: This is a boat dive only. Boats may be launched from Ocean cove, Stillwater Cove or Timber Cove. the site sits one-quarter mile offshore between Timber and Stillwater Coves. In spring through fall the spot can normally be found by a patch of offshore bull kelp. Watch for currents and boat traffic.

A diver cruises along a wall of metridium anemones.

Timber Cove

A perfect place to relax and take in a weekend of diving is at Timber Cove, one of the most protected and one of the most diver-friendly spots along the North Coast. The steep-sided bluffs surrounding the cove are a beautiful sight to behold. This large cove was once the home of a dog hole port and lumber mill, but now caters to divers, fishermen, and others who want to enjoy the ocean.

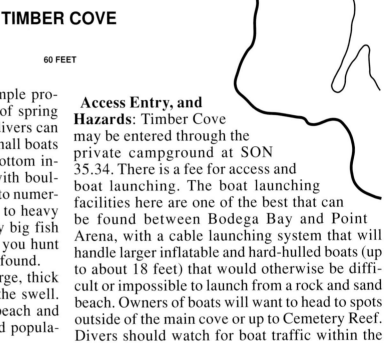

TIMBER COVE

The north wall of the cove offers ample protection from the northwesterly swell of spring and summer. Even during a big blow divers can still gain access to the ocean here in small boats or by swimming off the beach. The bottom inside of the cove consists of a rocks with boulders strewn about. These offer a home to numerous small fish and invertebrates. Due to heavy fishing pressure there are not as many big fish and abalone as there once was, but if you hunt around a bit there are still some to be found.

On the north side of the cove is a large, thick kelp bed that is well protected from the swell. This area is an easy swim from the beach and the rocky bottom still supports a good population of seven-to eight-inch abalone.

Better diving is found in the little coves both north and south of the main coves. The bottom here can be quite pretty, and some areas are covered with Metridium anemones, and others have a good selection of encrusting invertebrates. The variety of nudibranchs here is quite good. Here divers and fishermen will still find healthy populations of both game fish and abalone.

Access Entry, and Hazards: Timber Cove may be entered through the private campground at SON 35.34. There is a fee for access and boat launching. The boat launching facilities here are one of the best that can be found between Bodega Bay and Point Arena, with a cable launching system that will handle larger inflatable and hard-hulled boats (up to about 18 feet) that would otherwise be difficult or impossible to launch from a rock and sand beach. Owners of boats will want to head to spots outside of the main cove or up to Cemetery Reef. Divers should watch for boat traffic within the cove, and big waves and surge at the exposed points of the cove. You may avoid the day use fee by parking in the turnout at SON 34.55. The trail leads to the south point of Timber Cove (also known as Windermere Point or Kolmer Gulch).

The Timber Cove Boat Landing and Campground (phone: 707-847-3278) sits at the top of a bluff overlooking the cove, and the 30 campsites have a good view of the cove. Hot showers, trailer hookups, a laundry, telephones, and a store that rents or sells diving and fishing gear are available.

Those looking for a little more creature comforts may want to check out one of the cabins rented by the boat landing. Most have fireplaces or hot tubs and offer plenty of seclusion, but easy access to the ocean. There is also the Timber Cove Lodge for more conventional, upscale rooms and a good restaurant. Call 707-847-3231 for reservations.

Timber Cove.

Fort Ross State Historic Park

During the early 1800s the Russian fur hunters made their way down the coast and established a stronghold at Fort Ross. They built a small fort with stockade surrounded by a village that was so well fortified that the Spanish dared not attack.

By 1841 the otters were cleaned out all the way to the Channel Islands and the Russians sold everything (fort, houses, land; everything from Fort Ross To Bodega Bay) to John Sutter from Sacramento for $30,000. It was rumored that John never paid the Russians all that they were due. Later the fort became a cattle ranch and potato farm, then a sawmill and finally a dairy and sheep ranch. For years it was a port where dog hole schooners were loaded and unloaded from a high wire on the west point. Some chain and anchor points from the wire may still be found on the bluff above the western point of the cove.

The California Landmarks League purchased the land in 1903 sending it on its way to become the state historic park that it is today. The state has reconstructed the old fort and has turned it into a museum. Here, one can see photographs and artifacts of a bygone era. The Indian, the Russian, the lumberman, the farmer, and the seaman have all left their mark in Fort Ross. The one creature that has left little to mark its impact on the area is the cuddly sea otter. Exterminated from this part of the coast by over hunting, the only thing the otter has left are a few pelts hanging in the museum. Perhaps that is enough to teach the visitors of the fort a lesson that, hopefully, will not be easily forgotten.

Fort Ross Cove itself consists of two coves. An access road allows divers to drop off gear in the eastern cove, although parking is allowed only in the large lot on the bluff. The eastern cove has one of the few sand beaches in the county and is an easy place to launch inflatable boats or kayaks. This south-facing cove is well protected from the predominant northwesterly winds and is warm and sunny, particularly during the fall and winter months. The eastern cove is pretty well picked over of fish and abalone; however, there is a good population of eight-inch abalone on the eastern rim of the cove and on the rock piles that separate the eastern from western coves in fifteen to thirty feet of water.

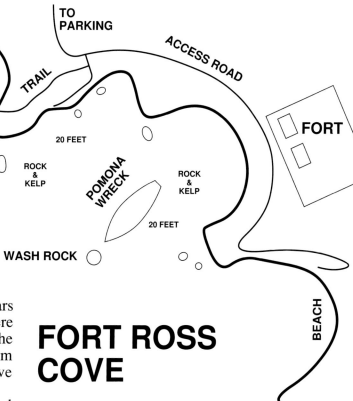

FORT ROSS COVE

The western cove is the more protected of the two, but it is only accessible by a steep foot path or from a boat launched from the eastern cove. The thick bed of bull kelp is home to assorted species of rockfish, with huge schools of blue rockfish being the most common. The boulder-strewn beach is a popular spot for harbor seals to haul out and sun themselves. Along the western point of the cove is a fair population of legal-sized abalone in 15 to 20 feet of water, and both the quantity and size increase as you get nearer the point.

The cove itself is fairly flat with rock and sand bottom getting no deeper than about 25 feet. Outside the cove the water drops down 60 feet to a garden of white plume anemones. Among the anemones may be found a few small cabezon and an occasional red octopus. Less frequently, divers chance upon a giant octopus. These octopus can reach some eight feet, tip to tip but are very shy, and divers often fail to notice these well-camouflaged creatures.

The best diving in the area is off of the western point itself. Divers who are in good physical shape may want to hike along the trail to the north point of the cove. The area may also be accessed by swimming around the point from the western cove or by launching a boat from the eastern cove. Here one can find a highly textured bottom with caves, canyons, and large boulders. Giant green anemones form clusters on the bottom in sunlit areas and rose anemones dot the bottom. The roofs of overhangs and caves in five to fifteen feet of water are adorned with both rose and Metridium anemones. There is a larger-than-average cave at the cut in the tip of the point that measures about ten by ten by thirty feet, and is beautifully decorated with orange and yellow sponges and an assortment of anemones. The water surrounding the point is covered with bull kelp and a good population of eight inch abalone among the rocky nooks and crannies from ten to thirty feet of water. Free-divers should be careful as the kelp in this area can be very thick.

Many ships have met their demise at Fort Ross, most notably the *Pomona* in 1908. The Schooner *J. Eppinger* also sunk here on December 30, 1899 while loading lumber as did the Schooner *Joseph F. Spinney* on October 27, 1893. The fishing boat *Riga* also went down here in modern times. Except for the *Pomona*, these were all wooden-hulled vessels and little remains of them today, although an occasional artifact is found. Divers must remember that the park and the waters surrounding it are an historical area, and no artifacts may be removed or harmed.

Access, Entry, and Hazards: Access is through Fort Ross State Historical Park at SON 33.00. Divers may drop their gear off at the beach and park in the large lot on the bluff. Inflatable boats and kayaks may be launched from the sand beach. Divers may hike along a trail to the western cove or the north point and down the bluff to the water. There is a day use fee. Should you wish to avoid the day use fee at the Historic Park you may park at the turnouts at SON 33.40 or 33.69, and take the longer trails to the point north of the Fort Ross West Cove.

Divers should note that the west point is diveable on only the calmest of days as it is directly exposed to the ocean swell. On calm days it is possible to enter directly off of the point; however, when the swell picks up swimming around from the cove is your only option. When the northwesterly wind and swell really picks up it's best to watch the giant breakers safely from shore. Divers should not enter any of the caves during a good swell to avoid being bounced around on the rocks.

Blue rockfish.

SS *Pomona*

On St. Patrick's Day in 1908 Captain Charles Swanson and the steam ship *Pomona* headed north out of San Francisco toward their moment in history. The *Pomona* was a deluxe, steel-hulled passenger freighter, 225 feet long and some 33 feet wide. She was fitted with twin boilers, 11 1/2 feet in diameter and 11 feet long, with a triple expansion engine having cylinders of 23, 36, and 56 inches in diameter. The *Pomona* topped out at 14 knots during her trial runs, quite fast by the standards of the time.

The *Pomona* was a show piece of the San Francisco waterfront and was outfitted with expensive hardwood panels of superb workmanship. What really made her stand out was that she was one of the first ships on the West Coast to be fitted with the newfangled Edison incandescent lamps along the deck and in the first class cabins. The *Pomona* appeared as a floating city at night to the awe of all who saw her, and was considered a great credit to the thriving waterfront business of San Francisco. For 20 years she plied the water between San Francisco and Eureka, carrying 200 passengers at a time and some light cargo.

On her last voyage she steamed north from San Francisco in the early morning hours. It was a clear day with a bit of wind and chop so the captain decided to hug the beach all the way up the coast. He plotted a course a little too long before turning out to avoid the Fort Ross Reef. One passenger remarked that he could identify the colors of the cows as they cleared the farm at the mouth of the Russian River.

Just before suppertime the *Pomona* hit the Monterey Rock (see Monterey sidebar), which was not marked by a buoy and was not marked on the charts of that time. The ship began taking on water and the captain decided to beach her at Fort Ross. The captain saw two buoys and, thinking that they were channel markers, headed right between them. In reality they were the marker buoys of a submerged mooring for the high wire that was used to load and unload ships. The *Pomona* hit another rock in the middle of Fort Ross Cove and never left the spot. The ship quickly filled with water, while the crew and passengers were safely taken ashore.

Salvage began almost immediately and some 150 tons of cargo were removed from the wreck, including seven trunks of expensive rugs. Afterwards, the local sheriff spent some time searching for the carpets after they were stolen from the beach. There was an attempt to refloat the *Pomona*, but before the work was finished, she broke up in a heavy swell. The *San Francisco Call* ran an article describing the salvage attempt, including a life-and-death struggle between one of the hard-hat divers and an enormous devilfish (an octopus?).

After the sinking of the *Pomona*, the Monterey Rock was marked with a whistle buoy, and to this writer's knowledge the *Pomona* was the rock's last victim. As asphalt roads and rail penetrated the North Coast, the need for ships waned and nobody hugged the beach anymore. The whistle buoy was later replaced with a simple marker buoy.

Today, little remains of the once proud ship. She sits in 15 to 25 feet of water just inshore from the large wash rock in the center of the west side of Fort Ross Cove. The two boilers and chain box are pretty much intact as well as the long propeller shaft. Otherwise the wreck is a scattered mass of metal plates, not much to look at but the wreckage a great hiding place for rockfish and red abalone. This site is more popular as a fishing spot than a wreck dive.

Nearly a century underwater has taken their toll on the wreck. Much of the iron has turned to rust and the hull collapsed many years ago. A heavy layer of marine algae covers the remaining parts and it is difficult to tell wreckage from rocks. A blow from a hammer or abalone iron easily distinguishes rock from wreck by the sound of metal ringing underwater. Smaller artifacts can be found by those with a little patience and a willingness to fan the sandy areas inshore of the main wreckage.

This is a historic wreck and no artifacts may be removed. The site is being studied by an archeological team, and may be declared a National Monument

Fort Ross Reef

Old timers remember this site as the Red Barn since it was behind the only red barn along this part of the coast. In fact, it was the only barn on the west side of Highway 1 on this part of the coast. Recent owners have broken with tradition and now a large white barn marks the dive site. The "Red" Barn is located at SON 31.00. At one time divers could access the beach via a trail behind the barn. Now divers may get to the beach through the campground or several state-owned trails. The state of California has bought up much of the land both north and south of the old barn and has given the area its own name, the Fort Ross Reef Campground. Those of us who have been diving here for more than a few years still call it "Red Barn".

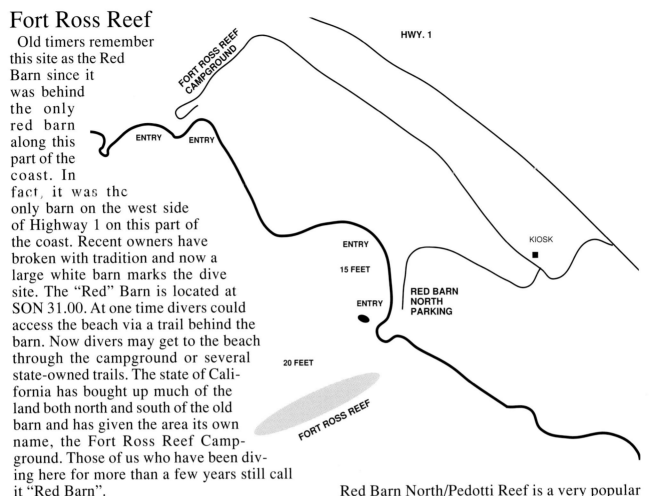

The most northerly entry is through the state-operated Fort Ross Reef Campground. Turn off Highway 1 at SON 31.37 and follow the road to the right to the Kiosk, pay the fee, and follow the road through the campground to a parking area near the water. There are several little coves at the road's end where you can enter the water. This is the easiest place to get to the water but the area has the worst diving. Few abalone and fish, and a not-so-interesting bottom may be found here.

The coastline at Fort Ross.

Red Barn North/Pedotti Reef is a very popular location due to the shore picking availability and was once the site of the Pedotti Ranch. Divers may reach the beach through at the Fort Ross Reef Campground at SON 31.37. First pay your fee at the kiosk and proceed through the gate west of the kiosk, keep left and park where the dirt road dead-ends. Follow the trail down the bluff and along the point to the left. The rocky area is Pedotti Reef. At low tide you'll see a lot of shore-pickers here. Good abalone diving is found on either side of the point. There are some fish worth spearing as well. Instead of heading left, many follow a trail to the right for access to shallow water with numerous small, but legal, abalone.

Red Barn South/The Longest Yard/Sheep Ranch is another popular location for shore-pickers. Park at the gate at SON 30.64. There are two ways to the water. Pass through the northerly gate and follow the trail across the meadow and down the gulch. The last part of the trail is steep but ends up on a gravel beach. Otherwise, you can pass through the south gate and follow the long dirt road to the beach. You will see why this is called the Longest Yard on your way back up.

SS Monterey

The *SS Monterey* was typical of dog hole schooners of the late 1800s. She had a wooden hull, was 120 feet long, had a 27-foot beam, drafted 8 feet, and displaced 382 tons. She had a steam engine, but was also rigged with two masts and sails. The *Monterey* was built in 1869 for Goodall, Perkins and Company, and was refitted in 1879.

On the evening of May 24, 1880, she left San Francisco and headed north. A strong northwest wind was encountered off Point Bonito, and the wind continued past 10:15 p.m. when the ship passed Point Reyes. The *Monterey* cleared the mouth of the Russian River about one mile offshore at about 2 a.m., the sails were lowered. Captain Von Helms left orders to "hog to the beach" to give his passengers a smoother ride and laid down for a nap at 2:30 a.m.

No sooner had the captain closed his eyes when the ship struck an unchartered rock about three miles south of Fort Ross. The captain was on deck in an instant and observed the ship's bottom floating alongside the *Monterey*. Fortunately, she did not stick hard and floated free of the rock.

Captain Von Helms did the only thing he could under the circumstances and looked for a sandy area to beach his ship. He found one just inshore of the rock, and ran the *Monterey* aground. All passengers and crew, along with everyone's baggage, made it safely ashore.

The rock that the *Monterey* struck was named the Monterey Rock after the incident and the prominent cut in the coastline where the ship was beached still goes by the name "Monterey Bend." This is the beach divers refer to as "South Red Barn." There is not much left of the *Monterey* today, just a few metal parts and two names on the map.

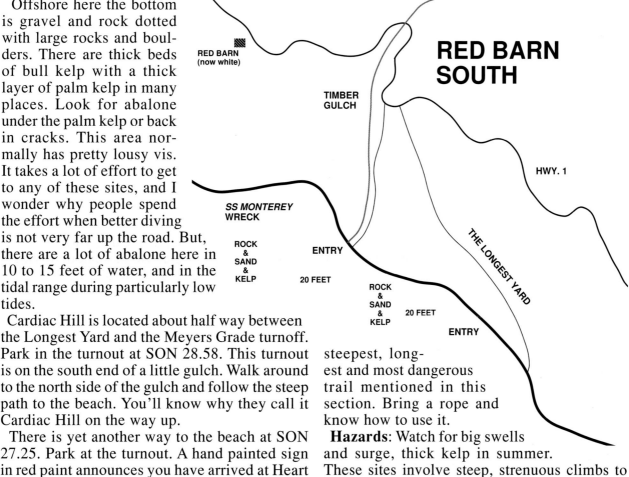

Offshore here the bottom is gravel and rock dotted with large rocks and boulders. There are thick beds of bull kelp with a thick layer of palm kelp in many places. Look for abalone under the palm kelp or back in cracks. This area normally has pretty lousy vis. It takes a lot of effort to get to any of these sites, and I wonder why people spend the effort when better diving is not very far up the road. But, there are a lot of abalone here in 10 to 15 feet of water, and in the tidal range during particularly low tides.

Cardiac Hill is located about half way between the Longest Yard and the Meyers Grade turnoff. Park in the turnout at SON 28.58. This turnout is on the south end of a little gulch. Walk around to the north side of the gulch and follow the steep path to the beach. You'll know why they call it Cardiac Hill on the way up.

There is yet another way to the beach at SON 27.25. Park at the turnout. A hand painted sign in red paint announces you have arrived at Heart Attack Hill. Follow the very steep and very long trail down the ridge and to the beach. This is the steepest, longest and most dangerous trail mentioned in this section. Bring a rope and know how to use it.

Hazards: Watch for big swells and surge, thick kelp in summer. These sites involve steep, strenuous climbs to and from the beach.

Russian Gulch

Most divers are in a hurry to get up Highway 1 to their favorite site, even though the coastline is rather spectacular and the curvy road does its best to slow them down. Just north of Jenner, Highway 1 makes a hairpin turn that will slow down all but the most determined sports car. Even if you have never stopped to enjoy the view or dive here, you probably recognize the curve as it adorns many postcards. The image is titled "Dramamine®️ Drive," and the hairpin curve marks Russian Gulch, the most southern of the semi-popular dive sites in Sonoma County. The site takes its name from the Russian farm and vineyard that occupied the site in the early 19th century. This was the first attempt by white men to colonize the area, and the first example of coastal agriculture along the West Coast.

Somewhat later the cove was known as Jenner Landing, after a family who operated a ranch at the mouth of the Russian River. In 1874 John Rule began to build a mill on the South Fork of Russian Gulch, but died before it was completed. His son, Charles took up the challenge and finished the task. Charles never used Russian Gulch Cove as a landing, but instead built his landing in the little triangular cove just south of Russian Gulch. This little cove was, and is still, known as Rule's Landing. Rule's Landing proved to be just a little too tricky to use and was abandoned. Rule built another landing at Russian Gulch and constructed a slide chute on the south side of the cove. He operated the mill until about 1900 and then gave the whole thing up to become a cattle rancher.

A few years later a Mr. Davis built a mill at the present site of the town of Jenner on the Russian River. Davis built a railroad connecting the mill and Russian Gulch and logged up the gulch and Russian River as far as he could. Some of the lumber was floated up river to the rail station at Markham, but most went out under the wire at Russian Gulch. The landing, by the way, always went by the name Jenner. Davis' mill closed down in the early 1900s, but H.A. Richardson continued to use the landing to ship lumber from his mill at Stewart's Point. After the sinking of Richardson's ship *Newberg* in 1918, the landing was finally abandoned.

Russian Gulch is now a unit of the Sonoma County state beaches and offers public access to this unimproved area. The visibility here is not as good as points north due to the outfall from the Russian River and the sandy, inshore area. It does shorten the drive for those wanting to pick their limit of abalone and head back to the Bay Area for supper. Offshore the bottom consists of rock and sand. Abalone here are plentiful and larger than average size. Fish are scarce.

Access, Entry, and Hazards: Park along Highway 1 at SON 24.50, just south of the famous hairpin curve and follow the trail to the beach. The wide sandy beach is a good place to launch kayaks to explore points north and south of the cove. Watch for big surf and swell. Rodney Ore was bitten by a white shark here while free-diving.

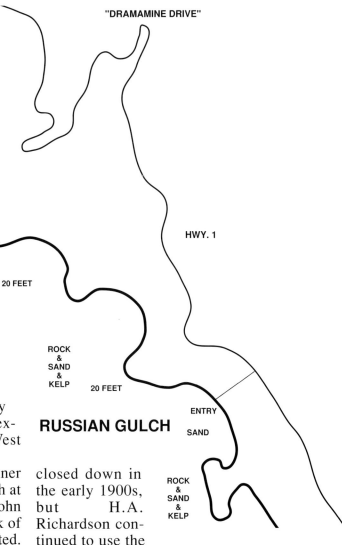

"DRAMAMINE DRIVE"

HWY. 1

ROCK & SAND & KELP

20 FEET

ROCK & SAND & KELP

20 FEET

ENTRY

SAND

RUSSIAN GULCH

ROCK & SAND & KELP

A diver moves in on some abalone.

Introduction to the San Francisco Bay Area

The Coastal Miwok and Ohlone Indians were the first to settle along the San Francisco Bay. The Miwok called the entrance to what we now call San Francisco Bay, "Yulupa," the place of the sun sinking into the ocean. The name "Golden Gate" was given to the entrance of San Francisco Bay in 1848 by a John Charles Fremont. Fremont, of course, knew nothing about the impending discovery of gold, but named the bay entrance after the harbor entrance of Constantinople, which was called the "Golden Horn."

Golden Gate Bridge.

Spanish farms began to spring up in the 1770s, and the Spanish built a mission they named "Mission San Francisco de Assisi." Captain William A. Richardson established a trading post at what he called Yerba Buena Cove in 1835. The outpost was a center to exchange hides and tallow for manufactured goods and was visited by British, Russian, and American ships. Later in 1846 the American flag was raised at Yerba Buena and the city was renamed San Francisco.

The coastline between Sonoma and Monterey Counties is considered by many to be a diver's wasteland—lots of sand and not much else. True, the area does have more than its share of sandy bottoms, and the outfall from Tomales and San Francisco Bays do mess up the visibility. However, the area does offer some good local diving for those without the time to head to either to Sonoma or Monterey Counties. Notably, this area offers fascinating opportunities for speciality diving and spectacular diving around offshore islands.

The diving around Point Reyes National Seashore is plagued by bad visibility, but is home to some of the most productive abalone beds and fishing grounds in all of California. Few divers enter the water here, more out of the fear of shark attack than considerations of access or visibility. Large colonies of pinnipeds along the seashore attract a sizable population of great white sharks. However, many enjoy these waters without ever encountering a big shark.

While technically in San Francisco County, The Farallons lie 29 nautical miles due west of San Francisco. These islands have, simply, the finest diving in all of California. Seldom visited and even more rarely dived, this underwater habitat is wild and untouched. These Islands and surrounding waters make up the Gulf of the Farallones National Marine Sanctuary, and sanctuary rules offer some added protection to the islands and their inhabitants.

North of the Farallons and west of Point Reyes lies a submerged pinnacle known as the Cordell Bank. The bank and surrounding waters are within the Cordell Bank National Marine Sanctuary, and while here is interesting diving here, the high spot is at 110 feet and much of the bank is considerably deeper. A description of this bank is out of the scope of this book because it is beyond the range of recreational divers. It has been well described in "Ecology of an Underwater Island" by Robert W. Schmieder, Cordell Expeditions, Walnut Creek, California (4295 Walnut Blvd., Walnut Creek, CA 94596).

San Francisco, San Mateo and Santa Cruz Counties all have numerous dive sites. Abundant game once created a following of advanced, local divers. These divers once regularly explored reefs around Pacifica, San Pedro, James V. Fitzgerald Marine Reserve, Pillar Point, Pigeon Point, Año Nuevo, and Natural Bridges. The game in these areas has long since been depleted and not even these rugged divers visit these reefs anymore. While on the rare day you may have a nice dive here, the diving regularly suffers from very bad visibility, strong currents and turbulent seas. Divers wishing pretty scenery should head south to Monterey or north to Sonoma and Mendocino Counties. At Año Nuevo State Reserve, huge numbers of elephant seals and California sea lions haul out during the winter and form breeding harems. Great white sharks lurk offshore awaiting for their favorite meal, an adult elephant seal. This was once a favorite site for divers to view large sharks from cages, but changes to the Monterey Bay National Marine Sanctuary rules put an end to this activity.

San Agustin

In the late 1500s King Felipe of Spain was concerned over the exploration of Sir Francis Drake in 1578. Even though the Pope clearly gave Spain the entirety of the Pacific Ocean, the King sent Sebastian Cermeno to what was then called Alta California to explore, locate and chart suitable harbors. Cermeno left on the *San Pedro*, but found his ship unseaworthy and leased the *San Agustin* in Manila.

On July 5, 1595 the *San Agustin* left Manila. The voyage was not without incident since the *San Agustin* was, apparently, not in much better shape than the *San Pedro*. The ship made landfall near Cape Mendocino (Humboldt County) and charted the coastline south.

Cermeno later anchored in Drakes Bay, and unloaded most of his men and a large longboat called a viroco. As many California seamen know, many of the anchorages on the North Coast are reasonably well protected from a northwesterly blow but get nasty real quick when the wind turns out of the south. Well, that is just what happened to Cermeno. With only a handful of crew on board, and while Cermeno and most of the crew watched helplessly from shore, the wind switched and drove the *San Agustin* on the beach and broke her to pieces. The crew salvaged what they could, piled bales of silk neatly on the beach, and 26 men rowed south in the viroco. Cermeno continued charting the coastline along the way and named the blight south of Point Reyes "La Bahia de San Francisco," although he never discovered the large bay that lurked behind the coastal hills. Despite many hardships, all 26 men made it to Acapulco.

In all, some 130 tons of cargo went down with the *San Agustin*. Among them were bales of silk, beeswax, clothing, and three distinct porcelain patterns that were popular in Europe at that time. Sebastian Viscaino pulled into Drakes Bay in January 1603 and looked for the wreck and the silk that Cermeno stacked so neatly on the beach. He found nothing. The local Indians had found their treasure.

Years later archaeologists from the University of California at Berkeley and Los Angeles dug through 17th century Indian grave sites and found iron rods, iron spikes and porcelain shards from the *San Agustin*. Even today big storms will bring a bit of porcelain up on the beach. This wreck site is currently being excavated by archaeologists, and it is considered one of California's most historic shipwrecks.

Point Reyes Area

Point Reyes sits on the seaward side of the San Andreas Fault and is gradually moving northward about one-half inch per year. The last big movement occurred in 1906 when the epicenter near Olema jumped some 20 feet. In the pre-European period, Point Reyes was home to at least 113 coastal Miwok Indian villages. The Point itself was named by Sebastián Vizcaíno in 1603 as Punta de los Reyes (Point of the Kings). What is now Point Reyes National Seashore became a ranch during the Spanish period. During the post gold rush the area provided a bit of timber, but mostly beef and hogs to the growing city of San Francisco.

Point Reyes saw more than its fair share of shipwrecks, and in 1870 a lighthouse was built some 300 feet above sea level. An automated light and foghorn were installed in 1975, but the original lighthouse and fresnel lens remain in place.

While much of the Point Reyes National Seashore is bordered by massive sandy stretches, there are a few good dive sites. The reef directly off Tomales Point begins as shallow rocks near the tip of the point and extends north for 200 yards to about 60 feet of water. In places the bottom consists of big rocks and mini-pinnacles. In other spots there is flat rock or sand.

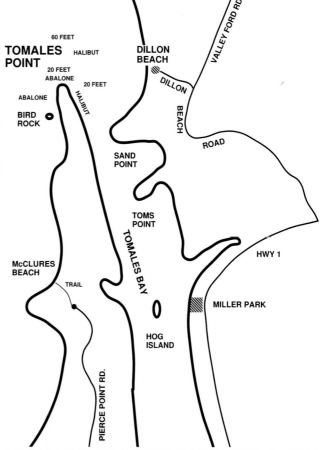

Flat sandy or rocky areas are a good spot to find halibut, and rockfish congregate around the rocks. Divers find many halibut along the 20-foot sand bottom on the inshore side of the point. The shallow water from the intertidal rocks down to 40 feet is a good place to hunt abalone.

Access, Entry, and Hazards: This site is accessible by boat only, and boats may be launched from Lawson's Landing at Dillon Beach; call 707-878-2443 for camping reservations or Miller Park.

The Abalone Point/Double Point area is located in the extreme southern end of Point Reyes National Seashore and is frequented by local abalone divers from Bolinas and Stinson Beach and by a few hard core divers who would like to experience all that California has to offer.

The bottom in the area consists of shale. The shale strata are slightly tilted, creating a saw-tooth pattern on the bottom. The shale is mostly smooth and with the area's generally rough conditions, it can support little in the way of encrusting invertebrates or algae; however, some does manage to survive.

At the edges of the shale strata the bottom is more textured and provides shelter for invertebrates. Abalone here are common and big. As a group this area has some of the largest, meanest abalone I have ever seen. Look for them in the crevices between shale layers. Often they are hanging upside down. On several outings the smallest abalone our group picked was over 9 inches and many were over 10.

This area is plagued by bad visibility due to the eroding bluffs above. Visibility is normally less than five feet and is often less than one. Abalone hunting here is done by the "Braille method."

Access, Entry, and Hazards: From Highway 1 take the Olema-Bolinas Road west toward Bolinas. Turn right onto Mesa Road and follow it toward the Palomarin Trailhead. About one-third mile before the Palomarin Trailhead is a parking area and a one-third mile trail that runs to the beach. Once on the beach, hike about two-thirds mile to the first of a series of points. The first is named Abalone point on the topographical map and the next two make up Double Point. Enter anywhere you like, but watch for big waves and surge. The Palomarin Trail runs along the bluff top and does not allow beach access for many miles. Should you choose to hike the trail, it ends up at the beautiful Alamere Falls. These falls are spectacular in winter and early spring and spill from the bluffs above to the beach.

NOONDAY ROCK

NORTH FARALLON

ISLE OF ST. JAMES

MIDDLE FARALLON

SOUTHEAST FARALLON

FARALLON ISLANDS

Farallon Islands

There is not much quality diving along the San Francisco coastline. However, some 29 miles west of the city are a group of islands that offer spectacular diving. The Farallon group consists of three major islands, many large rocks, and submerged pinnacles.

The lasting impression of the Farallon Islands is in the size and abundance of the marine life. Critters are not found here one or two at a time, but in huge aggregations. Each member of the group is near the maximum size that is observed for that species. These dive sites, in my humble opinion, offer the very best diving in all of California and are much better than many highly-rated, warm-water destinations.

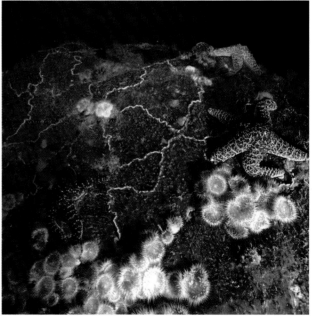

The wild colors of the Farallons.

Noonday Rock

At the far north end of the Farallon chain is Noonday rock, a submerged pinnacle marked by a whistle buoy. The name derives from the *Noonday*, a clipper ship who hit the rock and sunk in 1863. Noonday Rock was dynamited after the sinking but had to be marked by a buoy some years later because the seafloor here is steadily rising. The area around Noonday Rock is a raised plateau a half mile or more across. While much of the bottom in the area is between 100 and 200 feet deep, there are numerous high spots.

The high point at Noonday Rock is about 18 feet deep, and drops off steeply to the north and south. There are two small peaks with a steep valley in between. Under one peak is a deep overhang in about 80 feet of water that goes back some 20 feet. The crevasse is filled with China and vermilion rockfish. Invertebrate life here is outstanding with nudibranchs, anemones, and sponges. Hydrocoral at this location is sparse.

Another high spot we called Alan's High Spot after Captain Allen Cull. This area has a relatively flat top at 70 feet that is deeply carved with canyons. The rock then plunges with vertical walls on all sides to depths well beyond a diver's limit. The topography is similar to Farnsworth Bank off Catalina.

The marine life here is incredible. Thick schools of blue and black rockfish, and sardines hover above the rock. The rock itself is covered with a rich coat of color. Strawberry anemones and hydrocoral are the predominant invertebrates here, but rock scallops the size of serving platters are everywhere. This is one of the nicest collection of large hydrocoral trees I've ever seen. Wolf-eels inhabit many of the rocky crevices, and giant Pacific octopuses were found resting on top of the pinnacle. These were true giants with an arm span of nearly 10 feet.

Sami's Wall has a high spot at 50 feet and dropped off steeply to 150 feet. Lots of hydrocoral and big fish are found here.

Access, Entry and Hazards: This site is accessible only by boat. The rock does not break the surface and is marked by a whistle buoy. The buoy is not located at any of the high spots. The 18-foot high spot is at 37° 47.586' N, 123° 09.946' W (depths 20 to 150 feet). Alan's High Spot may be found at 37° 47.699' N, 123 10.433' W (depths 70 to 150 feet). Sami's Wall is at 37° 47.690 N, 132° 10.296' W (depths 50 to 150 feet). Watch for big seas, strong currents, and white sharks.

Noonday

The *Noonday* was a clipper ship some 200 feet long with a 38-foot beam, and displaced 2100 tons. She was built in New England for the California trade. On her maiden voyage in 1855 she made the trip from Boston, around the Horn, to San Francisco in 139 days. The trip went without incident as did her second trip. During her third voyage she struck a rock near the Banda Islands and was repaired.

On her forth and final voyage, she left Boston with $450,000 worth of general merchandise and headed for San Francisco. She had been at sea for 139 days on January 2, 1863 and Captain Henry and crew were eager to get their feet on dry land again. The seas were calm and the sky was clear. With a good breeze behind her she was at rigged at full sail and was making nine to ten knots. The Captain had nothing to worry about as she sailed over Fanny Shoal, North Farallon could clearly be seen some three miles away and there were no known navigation hazards on this shoal.

Captain Henry's optimism came to a screeching halt when the *Noonday* impaled herself on a shallow rock on Fanny Shoals. The ship began to sink immediately and is was fortunate that the pilot boat *Relief* could be seen about two miles away. The captain headed the *Noonday* toward the *Relief*, but did not get very far before she began to take on water. Lifeboats were lowered and all of the crew safely left the *Noonday* and were picked up by the *Relief*. The *Noonday* went down in 240 feet of water and could not be salvaged.

On modern nautical charts the high point at Fanny Shoal now carries the name "Noonday." The rock was chartered and dynamited after the sinking.

Zoanthid anemones.

Isle of Saint James

The bottom around North Farallon drops steeply from the island and we never found a suitable anchorage. However the waters around the Isle of St. James, just south of North Farallon Island provided us with spectacular diving. This is not a single island but a group of three islets and assorted rocks that form a semi-circle. In the center of the semi-circle is a protected anchorage that makes a good dive spot even when the wind and seas are up.

Most boats anchor in 70 feet of water on the lee of a massive, rocky reef. The reef begins at the water surface, drops gradually to 25 feet and then plunges vertically to 70 feet. Among the wall are schools of blue and black rockfish, numerous rock scallops, and huge numbers of urchins. Wolf-eels inhabit cracks at the base of the rocky wall. As many as 10 animals may be found in a small area.

The most colorful diving here is on the west side of the southeast islet. A rocky ridge begins in deeper water and runs up to a little wash rock on the northernmost point. The bottom is highly textured with steep-sided valleys and rock piles. Many of the rocks are covered with encrusting hydrocoral. Purple rocks would be a good name for this dive site since the intense color is simply overwhelming. Among the coral are huge numbers of nudibranchs, sea stars, aggregating and giant green anemones.

The small, northernmost wash rock on the southeast islet marks the entrance to an extensive cave system. This wash rock is actually a pillar that holds up the roof of the north entrance to the cave. The cave then proceeds right and then straight through the islet, branching several times. At least one on the branches dead ends, while others terminate on the west and north side of the islets.

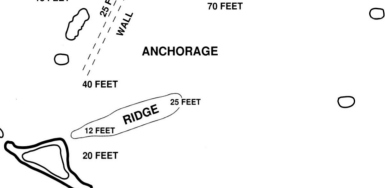

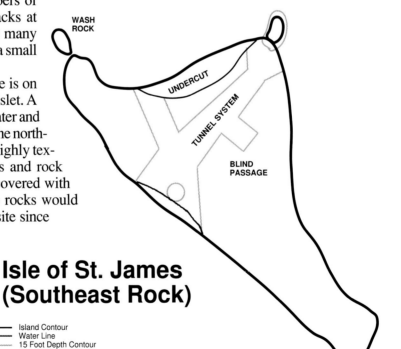

Isle of St. James
(Southeast Rock)

—— Island Contour
— Water Line
‒‒‒ 15 Foot Depth Contour

The interior of the cave is lined with invertebrate life—aggregating anemones, hydrocoral, and colorful sponges. There are also numerous snow-white, giant green anemones. See the description of these anemones in MacKerricher State Park description.

Access, Entry, and Hazards: Boat only. Anchor

in the protected area in the lee of the three large islets. This is the best anchorage outside of the Southeast Farallon Group.

Out from the Isle of St. James are several ridges that are hospitable to divers. Both are southwest of the islets at 37° 45.627' N, 123° 05.636' W., and at 37° 45.726' N, 123° 05.718' W. Both of these areas have a ridge top in 14 to 40 feet of water and drop off steeply on two sides. Wolf-eels, huge lingcod, and vermilion rockfish are everywhere. The area also has a colorful collection of sponges and anemones.

Middle Farallon

Middle Farallon is a tiny rock that barely breaks the surface, hardly big enough to be called an island. There is a nice wall that begins on the south side of the island and runs east-west. The invertebrate life here is very colorful. Huge red and orange sponges cover many rocks, and these are fed upon by red and orange nudibranchs. Large anemones dot the rocky wall. The wall is carved with many nooks and crannies, and these are home to many rockfish, cabezon, and wolf-eels. There are also many large rock scallops here.

Southwest Farallon

The South Farallon group consists of two major islands and several large rocks. Southeast Farallon is the largest of the two and is separated by the narrow Jordan Channel from Maintop Island to the west. Sir Francis Drake was probably the first European to set foot on the islands in 1579, and named the largest "Island of Saint James." Later Juan Francisco Bodega y Quantra gave the Islands its modern name of "Los Farallones de los Frayles" (the headlands of the friars) after the founders of the San Francisco Mission. The Farallons were not occupied until the middle of the 19th century when Russian fur traders, accompanied by Native American Indians, set up a outpost. In the process the Russians cleaned the islands out of their marine mammals.

During the Gold Rush Era there were no chicken farms near San Francisco and wild eggs had to do. A murre egg is about twice the size of a chicken's and is said to taste about the same. It is estimated that over 14 million murre eggs were harvested in the late 19th century. Of course, the bird population plummeted until 1911, when laws were passed to stop the egg harvesting and allow the bird populations to recover.

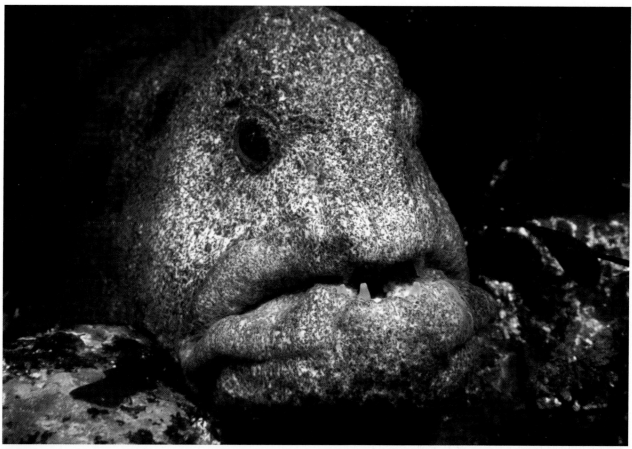

Wolf eel.

Henry Bergh

The *Henry Bergh* was a "Liberty Ship" built in the Kaiser Shipyards in Richmond, California in 1943. These were the famous ships turned out during World War II to ship supplies and troops around the world. Some 2710 of these simple and rugged ships were built and only 33 of these were outfitted to carry troops. The Henry Bergh was 441.15 feet long, had a 57-food beam, and displaced 7176 tons. She had facilities for 564 passengers.

On her last voyage she steamed out of Pearl Harbor for San Francisco, overloaded with 1300 sailors returning from the war and about 100 crew. As she neared the California she ran into a thick fog bank and steamed at 11 knots for 36 hours, without the opportunity to get a navigational fix.

Captain Joseph Chambers believed his ship to be 10 miles south of the Farallon Islands, but wind had pushed her about 10 miles northward. On the morning of May 31, 1944 a mate thought he heard a whistle but was unable to get a bearing due to the noise the celebrating sailors were making. At 5:00 a.m. the *Henry Bergh* ran onto the rocks about 200 yards offshore of the west end of Southeast Farallon Island. Even with her big, triple expansion engines in full reverse she did not budge off the rocks.

The ship's SOS reached San Francisco at 5:05 a.m. and help was immediately dispatched, but would not arrive until after 8 a.m. In the meantime the ship began to break up and the captain ordered the passengers ashore. The sailors were shuttled 25 at a time in 8 life boats. In all some 600 men had either been taken off the ship or had swam to shore before help arrived. It was remarkable that all of the passengers and crew made it off the ship alive. Only two were injured; thirty-five required hospitalization for exposure.

Captain Chambers and a few men remained on the ship and rigged a line, but she could not be pulled off the rocks. When it was clear that the ship was stuck for good the captain ordered his ship abandoned and was the last one off. At 4 p.m. a loud crack was heard across the water as the ship broke in two.

Later at the inquiry it was determined that Captain Chambers made errors piloting the vessel's course, proceeded at an unsafe speed through thick fog, failed to use navigational aids including soundings, and permitted his passengers to be so noisy as to interfere with the lookouts. The captain was demoted to first mate. The ship later broke up into three sections. The hull forward of the bridge washed up onto Southeast Farallon, and the bridge lay partially submerged, just offshore. The stern piece is hung up on a reef about 200 yards offshore. No salvage was ever attempted.

The first lighthouse was built on Southeast Farallon in 1853. It was accompanied by a unique wave-powered foghorn that took advantage of a blowhole and a cave system under the island. There were several lighthouses built on the island, and fire destroyed one after another. Today, an automated lighthouse still directs shipping into San Francisco Bay.

The Point Reyes Bird Observatory operates a year-round research station on the island, and these scientists are the island's only human residents. Birds, marine mammals, and white sharks are the object of the scientists study.

The bottom around Southeast Farallon consists of a near-shore rocky shelf in 20 to 40 feet of water, and then gradually drops off. The inshore bottom is covered with a jumble of large boulders. Algae covers most of the rocks and provides shelter for a host of invertebrates. Algae found here is not giant or bull kelp as neither of these long-stalked algae can survive the rough water here. The algae found here is the short, lettuce-like kelp.

Red sponge nudibranch laying eggs.

Around the boulders and under the layer of kelp are huge beds of abalone. Even prior to legislation in 1997 that prohibited the commercial and sport take of abalone South of San Francisco, the area still had an abundance of the tasty mollusks. It could be due to the often inhospitable weather that limited the number of diveable days, or the perceived threat of shark attack. Still, these reefs looked as if they had never seen an abalone diver.

Access, Entry and Hazards: These islands are accessible only by boat. Southeast Farallon is about a two-hour boat ride from Pillar Point Harbor. There are permanent mooring buoys at Fisherman Bay and Maintop Bay. Southeast Farallon is the largest and offers the best anchorages in the area. Divers should watch for strong currents, big waves and surge. This is a known white shark feeding area.

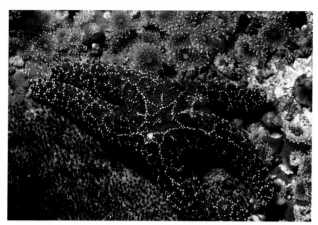
Ochre star.

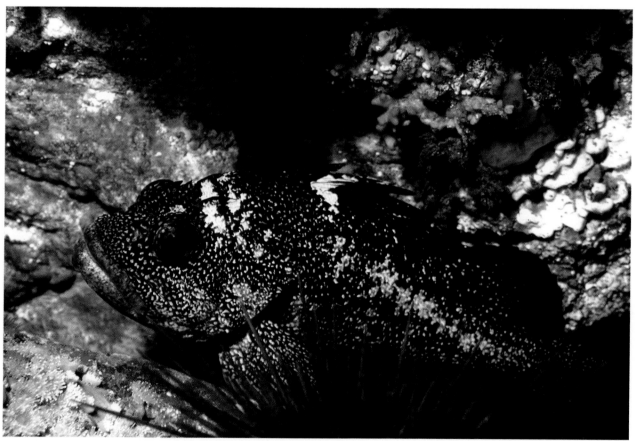
China rockfish.

Index